W9-AXG-350

DISCARDED

HOW TO SAVE YOUR OWN STREET

HOW TO SAVE YOUR OWN STREET

BY RAQUEL RAMATI

In collaboration with
The Urban Design Group of the
Department of City Planning
New York

Dolphin Books

Doubleday and Company, Inc.
Garden City, New York
1981

Dolphin Books
Doubleday & Company, Inc.
Library of Congress Catalog Card Number 78-14709
ISBN: 0-385-14814-3

THIS BOOK IS DEDICATED TO MY PARENTS GILA AND MICHAEL SCHANZ

ACKNOWLEDGMENTS

This book has been a joint effort of the Urban Design Group of the Department of City Planning of the City of New York, spurred on by the support of the City administration itself.

Special thanks are due to Mayor Koch and to Deputy Mayor Wagner for their continued encouragement. John E. Zuccotti, the former chairman of the Planning Commission whose pioneering work in neighborhood revitalization guided our work, was an inspiration to us all. Credit is also due to former Mayor John V. Lindsay who was the first to include the discipline of urban design in government work.

While the book reflects the creative energy of the entire staff of the Urban Design Group, there are several members who deserve special mention. Patrick Ping-tze Too was the project designer for the three case studies and played a major role in developing the book and, with Kuo-ming Tsu and Fred Lee, in preparing the graphics. Renée Kemp-Rotan, Lois Mazzitelli, Brunilda Mesa, and Merry Neisner were tireless in their research and their assistance in preparing the manuscript.

William Marlin, the architectural editor and critic whose writings in *The Christian Science Monitor* helped bring the news of our street-saving notion to the nation during the 1970s, provided invaluable editorial counsel. Paul Grotz, the designer of the book, demonstrated patience and creativity. My sincere gratitude to both.

Jacqueline Onassis, my editor, the first to recognize the importance of this project, supported it throughout; my warmest appreciation to her. And particular thanks to Lindy Hess for her humor and her editorial guidance and to Patrick Filley and Alex Gotfryd for their participation and advice.

I'm also grateful to Jack Dillon, Christopher Cross, C. Ray Smith, Gerry Helferich, John Hart, Kanubhai Vyas, Dorothy Svitzer, Dorothy Miner, Eva Anderson, Philip Wallick, Nina Rosenwald and to all the members of the Department of City Planning who contributed their talent and valuable time.

My thanks to the Design Arts Program of the National Endowment for the Arts, whose grant made this project possible.

To Saul Steinberg whose genius has given to all of us new insights into urban life, my deepest appreciation for the generous contribution of the cover drawing.

Finally, thank you to the people in the community who, over the course of many stormy meetings, convinced me of the value of incremental planning and inspired me to write this book.

CONTENTS

INTRODUCTION: Not Just a Road

Streets take up about a third of the land area in our cities. Yet many Americans think of streets as places to avoid or endure, not as places to enjoy and remember.

The most obvious reason for this waste is that cars, buses, and trucks dominate the street and often seem more important than people. Fortunately, this is not a completely accurate image. Many streets, such as those this book portrays, have yet to be reduced to mere roads, and increasing numbers of people are determined to keep their streets from such a fate.

This book is about saving the kinds of streets that thread through thousands of retail and residential neighborhoods across the country. They tie together the physical characteristics, social activities, and cultural resources of our immediate surroundings. Saving your own street, turning neglect around and beating back blight, is a way of taking part in some very practical pioneering.

In the context of a dawning urban renaissance, new realities emerge.

First, the nation's urban policies have, in recent years, begun to emphasize the revitalization of existing neighborhoods. Streets are their core and countenance. Making sure that streets take on a new life is basic to this neighborhood strategy.

Second, these neighborhoods and streets form existing resources. It is becoming clear that we all have a stake in making the most of what exists — conserving and improving upon and maintaining investments made over the years. Streets, not to mention the buildings edging them, are a reflection of such past expenditures. Caring for them, we conserve a reflection of ourselves, of our fellow citizens, and of a shared cultural heritage.

Third, no one else is going to undertake and pay for this process unless you (''you'' here, and throughout the book, refers to an owner of a building along the street, a community leader, a government planner, a city commissioner, an architect, a real estate developer seeking a zoning change, or any individual or group having an interest in their street) take the lead, create a constituency, and learn how to tap the resources of both government and the private sector. The days of massive monetary infusions for expansive physical improvements seem to be over. The book explains how to draw upon the resources of government in times of fiscal caution and material constraint.

This is a practical book because it spells out the details and steps of the process — but not as a hard-and-fast, firmly etched template that can be laid over every neighborhood situation. Rather than locking anything in, the process described here is more like a flexible framework that can enable a process of your own to emerge.

Fourth, the book's emphasis on a small-scale approach shows how you can discern, and design for, the physical possibilities of your street while at the same time maintaining a distinctly human focus. The stories of the streets told in this book — Mulberry Street in Little Italy, on Manhattan's Lower East Side; Newkirk Plaza, in Brooklyn; Beach 20th Street, in Far Rockaway, Queens — are about enterprises small enough to be manageable by the neighborhoods that were directly involved. This level of scale allows a more effective channeling of local energy and emotion. The scale of a street relates not only to a collection of buildings, but also to a community of interests. And the scale of your own street-saving process must ensure that these interests, in all their diversity, are involved as much as possible.

Given a place as physically, socially, and politically complex as New York City, it may seem at first that the three street stories told here are a bit removed from your own situation. Yet Mulberry Street, Newkirk Plaza, and Beach 20th Street are really the cores of "small towns." Packed into New York City's vast network, such havens of human scale abound. In their physical properties, and especially in their mix of people and functions, these streets are not all that different from the more familiar "main street" in cities of many sizes. This book tells about streets where there is still a retail, residential, or cultural edge to hold on to. Streets where there are people who care and whose determination has already led them to form a community-interest group, can be salvaged through concerted effort. These kinds of streets are typical in cities of many sizes, with people protecting them with zeal.

Our streets must be thought of as more than just roads. They are, in fact, multidimensional spaces with many overlapping functions. The street is a latticework of links for various modes of transportation and, in the richest sense, for various kinds of pedestrian activities. The street is bordered by buildings and, when those borders are especially alluring, they have a mix of shops, stores, restaurants, or handsome entrances to residential units.

Such streets are the "living rooms" of their neighborhoods. They are centers for human interaction where people meet, where work, leisure, and shopping converge, where day and night mesh into a round-the-clock hub of life and communication.

In *How to Save Your Own Street,* we suggest ways to enlist the energies, skills, and cooperation of the community — from its merchants, businessmen, and bankers to its educational institutions, governmental agencies, and design professionals and artists.

This book will provide information about streets from the technical to the historical, and in the process you will gain an understanding of how a street relates to the more general area around it. From such information and its impact, one can move into the planning procedures by which the potential of a street can be gauged, alternative design proposals spelled out, the support of the community secured, and an overall improvement program launched.

Learning about the neighbors who got things started on Mulberry Street, Newkirk Plaza, and Beach 20th Street may help one learn something about one's own neighbors as well: uncovering assets of the street that may have been taken for granted or that may have been obscured over the years by sloppy modernization, bad upkeep, or environmental chaos.

How to get started — from thinking through a realistic budget, to securing assistance in the form of expertise and financing, to the importance of maintenance, is also pointed out.

And to help ensure that your design improvements are protected and, still better, lead to long-term resurgence, we offer details about the innovative zoning techniques that have emerged in recent years. Laws and ordinances regarding the preservation of historic buildings, sites, and districts will be covered, along with their important funding implications. The ground swell of tax incentives to encourage a more thoughtful, people-oriented approach to new construction will be described. These sections are meant to provide a range of experiences and precedents.

The three street stories told in the book were developed, or one might say "coauthored," by the Urban Design Group of the New York Department of City Planning in close collaboration with the respective communities. The Group, set up in 1967, had a strong mandate to improve the physical quality of the city, and it built a record for fresh, inventive ways to achieve not only better aesthetics in architecture, but also public amenities as part and parcel of new development. In the mid-1970s, when New York City was facing a harsh budgetary crisis, the Group redirected its priorities from large-scale developments to small-scale projects — notably the street-saving ones described in this book. Within this tight economic atmosphere and a growing emphasis on community participation, it became apparent that such small-scale projects are becoming the core of economic revitalization, and more than just for superficial "beautification." While fostering a more positive relationship between the private sector and the city government, it went further to spur — not supplant — the public's role in instigating physical improvements.

The Group's approach to urban design placed as much importance on preserving existing noteworthy buildings as on reviewing major new developments. In setting up urban design criteria for plazas, subway stations, and sidewalk cafes, the Group advocated for pedestrian rights without neglecting the legitimate role of the automobile in the planning process. The Group has also worked out several special-zoning districts to preserve the scale and mix of activities of unique neighborhoods.

In New York there are formal advisory groups, called Community Planning Boards, who represent the community at large. While by mandate their role is advisory only; in fact, their political clout gives them a significant voice in all planning matters.

Most cities have some form of public access to planning decisions. Neighborhood councils are thriving in Minneapolis, Seattle, and San Diego. A "sunshine law" in Florida mandates public presentation of all proposed development, and in California major zoning matters are often referred to public referendum. Chicago's strong aldermanic system now allows for greater consultation with community groups. Boston has "little city halls," with planners attached to each. While the structure varies from city to city, a framework exists in every community for the citizens to articulate their own views and become equal partners in the street-saving process.

By getting involved, you will be reclaiming some of the fundamental spirit behind this country's origins and growth. It was on the street, with our feet shuffling on the courthouse square, that America discovered its identity and concentrated its drives. It seems impossible to think of any city or town in pioneering America that did not depend on at least one street as its "living room." The squares of Savannah or of New England, the wrought-iron balconies of New Orleans, the recessed arcades of Santa Fe, the narrow lanes of Boston's Beacon Hill all bring to mind the function of streets as places where values, not just vehicles, intermingle. Even the western settlers curled their Conestoga wagons into a circle around the campfires for company as well as protection — thereby creating an instant "public space" as historically vivid and valid as the most resplendent, urbane esplanade.

The advent of the automobile, the advance of technology and industrial processes, the spread of electronic communication — all promoted the proliferation of our cities. Functions that had long been closely packed along our streets, as symbolized by the old general store and post office, became increasingly dispersed. As urban sprawl galloped outward amid smaller cities and towns, older streets were gradually drained of their economic life, with retail and commercial activity clustered within plasticized shopping centers. We thought we had all the energy, gasoline, and acquisitive gumption we would ever need. Never would abundance be scarce.

We were wrong. And this lies at the bottom of why so many Americans, in cities and towns of all sizes, are turning to their streets once again. In the course of rejuvenating them, we are rejuvenating our basic human values and putting property values in a more mature perspective. Consumerism, community participation, environmental and energy awareness, the heightened accountability of corporations and industry, careening rates of inflation and interest—all are joining in an atmosphcrc more receptive to the thrifty stewardship of resources.

We hope that this book will inspire you to look at streets with a fresh eye and make them a vital, inviting factor in your daily life. The thrust here is not the creation of new streets, but the rekindling of existing ones; not the instant implementation of huge urban renewal projects, but carefully planned, incremental steps that can be taken right now—steps that can lead to improvements that are visible, affordable, and sustain community input. Such modest improvements, if they are

strategically located and timed, can lead to other, larger improvements—finally more meaningful because they will have been rooted in such a community spirit.

Street-saving is a journey that must be taken within a broader environmental, social, and economic context. But in this framework, a small scale and an incremental approach will help destine this journey to succeed. As Dostoyevsky put it, the most lasting forms of revolution take place one man at a time, and the same can be said of urban and community revitalization—one street at a time.

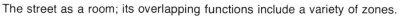

The street as a room; its overlapping functions include a variety of zones.

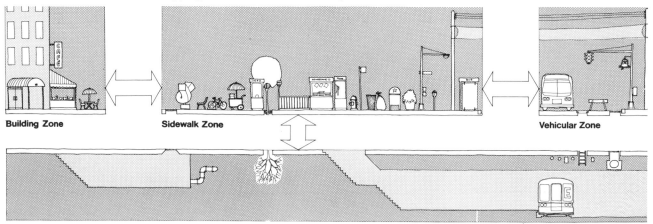

Building Zone   **Sidewalk Zone**   **Vehicular Zone**

Underground Zone

HOW TO SAVE YOUR OWN STREET

Three street projects will be discussed here—Mulberry Street, which runs through the Little Italy section of the Lower East Side of Manhattan; Newkirk Plaza, which is situated in Brooklyn; and Beach 20th Street, in the Far Rockaway section of Queens. Each street had unique problems, opportunities, and the potential for change. Yet in basic approach, they embody similar strategies. Motivated by common conviction, this approach can be put to work on just about every street in America.

There is no one sequence, final formula, or handbook for improving all streets. In New York City, the particulars were different from project to project. But there is a line of continuity that threads through any street-saving process as it unfolds. It is the first step of involving the community, early; herein lies the basis of change.

COMMUNITY INVOLVEMENT

Community involvement has become a catchphrase. But the fact is that you are going to be able to do something valuable for your street only with a sense of civic unity and shared enterprise. Getting a good cross section of community interest and opinions is essential to persuade various people of their common goal.

Every one of the three streets described here already had some framework for community cooperation, which is a basic assumption of the Urban Design Group's approach. If such a framework does not exist in your community, you have to create it—and you can.

A primary challenge is to excite people and engage their energy to join you in your new venture. Remind them that a street—their street—is a unifier. Emphasizing the street's role as a motivating force will help you draw people together.

The Community Is Your Client

It is necessary to have a client. The client in this context is the community. You should familiarize yourself with its needs, just as an architect who is designing a home must understand the desires and needs of a family.

An organized community can make several indispensable contributions during the start-up phase. Nobody knows a street quite as intimately as its inhabitants—including not only the people who actually live there, but also those who work there, who own businesses there, and everyone else who has a stake in the area. They can help you round up information and impressions—in effect, help you define the frontier. They know where the sunny and pleasant places are, and where the dark, unsafe corners are to be found. They will tell why and where people gather along the street and at what times of the day or which days of the week. If your project is ever going to come to fruition, these are the people whose input is essential and whom you will grow to depend on. In addition, when a constituency is rallied, it will be noticed by the community's political representatives, who will help your group to lobby for the seed money necessary for your plans to begin.

Regardless of how creative your eventual plan is, there is always the crucial task of keeping the momentum alive—seeing the process down the road, step by step—and the long-term responsibility of the physical maintenance of the street improvements. Community involvement is vital in this continuing process.

Identify Community Groups

Identifying who the community consists of is not always easy. In New York City, there are formally structured community groups and those that organize themselves sporadically around a cause. Organized groups include the Community Planning Boards, block associations, chambers of commerce, coalitions for social services such as the Community Service Society or cultural entities such as the Municipal Art Society. The more informal groups include residents, store owners, and students from nearby schools or universities, as well as shoppers and visitors.

Obviously, you are not going to be able to get as much direct help from people who are just passing through your street, or even working there, as you will from those who live or own property there. One of the first things you should do is to get both groups into the same camp, so that you have a single "client" to deal with. Remember that your street-saving process is indeed a unifier, a point of reference for these groups to convene for a common purpose.

In the process of widening participation, the community will have to decide whether the organizations that already exist adequately represent the street's various interest groups. Sometimes a *new* association will have to be started. An improvement process is a public undertaking: ideas and opinions must be shared by the various people who make up the "client" if the project is to be a success. Identify those people who represent different points of view, including those who may see a proposed improvement as some sort of threat. Leave out a group and you will regret it.

For example, in Little Italy, for which a special preservation zoning district was being created, the process was already well underway when it was discovered that the powerful, adjacent Chinese community was not being adequately represented. As a result of this realization, all improvements were restudied for an additional three months in order to get this group's participation, and eventually its consent, before the zoning measure passed.

Finally, human nature being what it is, there will always be those who are against everything. But you'll find many more people on your street whose concern for the community will be your largest source of strength. An organized community is one that is bound by awareness and caring.

Develop a Community Task Force

While you want as many people involved as possible, you certainly can't call several hundred people together for a decision on every detail. Instead, a task force should be formed that is small enough to be manageable, yet large enough to represent as many groups as possible. This task force can mobilize neighborhood resources. It will also become a forum for the discussion of alternate plans, and it will serve as a communication link between the planners and the entire community during the design process and the future implementation stages.

The formation of a task force can help the improvement plans get off the ground more quickly. It is important to give the community a feeling that something is happening right away. It may take weeks or months to repave a street, or to embellish it with landscaping and benches. But the task force can decide in twenty-four hours to close off the street to traffic, if only for a day or weekend. A street closing is a dramatic way to create excitement and festivity and to help people rediscover their street. At Newkirk Plaza, for instance, the community organized a crafts fair, called the "Made in Brooklyn League," which drew hundreds of people, whose interest, in turn, drew attention to the plaza's potential.

At Mulberry Street, a photographic exhibit of noteworthy buildings in the area was set up on a blank wall, right at the street's entrance. For many, the exhibit gave a fresh look at the neighborhood's best and renewed an interest in the street's architecture. Outsiders demonstrated their enthusiasm for Mulberry Street by organizing another exhibit at the McGraw-Hill Building in Midtown Manhattan. This is an important example of how people outside of your neighborhood can generate interest in your street and promote its needs.

Other examples show how a single action can inspire people to redirect their energy to improve their whole neighborhood. In Provincetown, Massachusetts, at the outermost reach of Cape Cod,

Provincetown, Massachusetts

the projected reconstruction of the Provincetown Playhouse-on-the-Wharf, where Eugene O'Neill wrote and performed his first plays, awakened the town to the importance of its literary, as well as physical, heritage. A public design-selection process for the new building required research into the cultural and architectural history of the town. On the old, water-edged street near the new theater, the study highlighted the contrast between the extraordinary Colonial, Greek Revival, and Victorian buildings and the sloppy development and garish signs of more recent decades. The Playhouse thus focused public attention on the quality of design — not just for the new building, but more vitally on the need to preserve the town's beauty and legacy.

In Marshall, Michigan, now in the process of being designated a national historic district, dozens of stores that were empty a few years ago are again occupied and economically vigorous. Its

Michigan Ave., Marshall, Michigan

main street has been conserved, its old squares spruced up, the signs on its buildings simplified and coordinated. This achievement stems from general public enthusiasm that was generated by a series of annual open houses of Marshall's Greek Revival, Gothic Revival, Second Empire, and Italianate residences. The process of exposure and education made people realize that Marshall's resources should not be limited to historic preservation, but should be redirected to include the town's main street and residential areas. In building interest in your own project, every effort — each exhibit, fair, or open house — should be thought of as an occasion to alert everyone, even the cynic, that this is the beginning of your street's transformation.

Do not overlook the help that the media can give you. You will find that most of the local newspapers and radio and television stations are eager to inform their communities that something creative and upbeat is taking place. Larger, nationally oriented newspapers such as *The New York Times*, *The Washington Post*, *The Wall Street Journal*, *The Christian Science Monitor*, and *The Chicago Tribune* regularly feature articles (even about places and initiatives far removed from their home bases) dealing with architecture, urban design, and community development. Do not hesitate to get the word around to reporters and critics that what you are doing not only has local importance, but also can offer practical lessons and human interest for a large regional or national readership.

You may also want to promote your own publication. In Milwaukee, for example, the Community Development program publishes an attractive monthly newsletter called *Focus*, which is sent to some 80,000 households free of charge. It describes specific neighborhoods, along with planning tools ranging from social services, such as day- and health-care, to rehabilitation strategies for building homes and businesses.

In Springfield, Massachusetts, a publication — its cover having the format of *Time* — captured the imagination of residents, business people, merchants, and public officials. The 100,000 copies distributed explained the city's downtown development processes and objectives and called upon people to pitch in and help.

Everyone Can Help

Involve as many community people as you can: children, college students, older citizens, and the owners of shops and restaurants can help you move from the level of ideas and aspiration to the day-by-day tasks of carrying out the real work. Don't underestimate the help of anyone who is willing to work. The very force of their caring gives the project a kind of momentum and, practically speaking, you need all the assistance you can get. Looking up facts and figures, photographing buildings, counting cars to get an idea of the volume of traffic along your street, recording the flow and concentration of pedestrians at various points are necessary tasks that can be handled by paraprofessionals.

You may also get lucky and find some community members who are willing to donate materials or provide them at cost. Perhaps your local nurseryman could provide trees, or the hardware store some paint. Others can volunteer their professional or trade skills: a bricklayer, a photographer, a landscape expert, or a graphic designer, all can be of invaluable help to you. Although you shouldn't count on such assistance as your main resource, you may be surprised at how many people will answer a call for help that is within their means, schedule, and ability. You may be amazed at the positive reaction you get from merchants' groups, local and state agencies, educational institutions, public officials, and the corporate community. Almost every major corporation or bank now has a public affairs program or an affiliated philanthropic activity. Corporations are eager to be asked to participate in meaningful projects, since it is in their best interest to build a positive image and provide better exposure for their business. Also, representatives of the corporate community tend to recognize and support enterprising people — like you.

Get Government Agencies and Politicians on Your Side

Put aside the notion that "you can't fight city hall"! Learning to maneuver within a city's bureaucracy and getting through the political system are essential in the process of saving streets.

If your city has a planning department at the local or regional level, there is a good chance that the staff members will help you once they recognize the merit of your proposal. City professionals in the fields of architecture, city planning, and urban design will contribute to your project and will help guide you through the labyrinthine network of local, state, and federal grants. Budget directors and policymakers will recognize that your project is eligible for available financial assistance and that it falls within government programs that provide grants for neighborhood improvement. In fact, small-scale, realistic projects with community backing are sought after by government officials. After all, they can be implemented quickly and become immediately visible.

New York City has a City Planning Commission with several local planning offices — and the centralized Urban Design Office. Most cities (and, increasingly, small towns) have similar bodies in charge of various physical improvements. If your city has such a department, you know where to start. Make a few calls to discover which section would be most responsive to street improvement and neighborhood revitalization.

Some cities have no such agencies. But don't give up easily if this is the case in your community. There will always be an individual — at the office of the building inspector, the zoning board, the land surveyor, or even the mayor — who can tell you which agency, or which group of agencies, is "in charge of streets."

If you are fortunate to have a planning agency, find out whether it is structured geographically or according to function, i.e., housing, education, parks, zoning, transportation, preservation, et cetera. For your endeavor, such functional divisions will frequently overlap. Talk to every division that might be affected by your project because you need their help. Create an atmosphere where all the agencies will cooperate. Approach them with diplomacy, and be attentive to each agency in order to develop a rapport. Make them major participants in your effort and they will work together with you.

For example, in Far Rockaway, on Beach 20th Street, the community wanted to widen the sidewalks but met resistance from several different interest groups. The Urban Design Group produced several alternate designs, addressing squarely the problems of each city department. Eventually, the government officials saw the benefits of widening the sidewalks and finally recognized the project's feasibility. The street-widening issue was the beginning of a new dialogue and cooperation between these agencies which thereafter worked together to support the concept.

Help from public officials will win the respect of your assemblyman, alderman, councilman, congressman, and senator. Besides being helpful in steering you to the right doors in city hall, these officials are veterans at organizing the community. They know where the local, state, and federal resources are, and they have a say in how funds are allocated. They also have a special interest in their constituency. One such official was responsible for getting $150,000 of state money for the Newkirk Plaza improvement; others helped to ensure start-up money for Far Rockaway.

Let whoever is trying to win votes in the neighborhood know what you are doing, what groups of people and interests are supporting you, and why the improvements will add to the popularity and profitability of the street. Don't be hesitant. Public officials have an interest because, sooner or later, they will be campaigning on that street of yours — or maybe even *because* of it.

Universities Are a Major Resource

You will find universities to be resourceful and willing sources of help, especially those with city-planning or architectural departments. Professionals and students in the nearby educational institutions, like the residents, are interested in making the neighborhood attractive. Students taking courses in planning or architecture will find your project a realistic "laboratory" for study. Today, they are being given more and more assignments dealing with actual urban problems, as part of the practical "school of life" approach. The dean of a school, or the faculty, may be delighted to help. Your street project may even become part of the curricular requirements.

Students are able to draw, do field work or analysis, and help define objectives and goals. They also bring a fresh and innovative point of view. They aren't limited by political realities and are willing to test unconventional ideas. Young people add an important dimension to the views of the professionals and the community. However, one must remember that they are students and that their primary responsibility is to their studies; limit their work to what they can handle.

In Biloxi, Mississippi, several teams of students from universities around the area worked with nationally known architects in coming up with designs for that city's new library and cultural center. In the process, they made recommendations for the city's overall development opportunities downtown. Another example is Lincoln, Nebraska, where a team of professors and students, in close consultation with the city and state governments, developed a comprehensive, well-detailed plan for improving the quality of the streets surrounding architect Bertram Goodhue's celebrated soaring State Capitol.

Also in Lincoln, in a joint venture between the city and the university, oral histories of six neighborhoods are recorded in a series of slide/tape shows. This information is the basis for depicting the role of design in each neighborhood, and is highlighted in posters displayed throughout the community.

There are literally hundreds of examples of this kind of institutional collaboration, and students of architecture are hungry for this type of non-theoretical challenge. Even McDonald's, golden arches and all, has invited the nation's architecture students to submit designs for the company's new facilities; the new designs might affect not only small retail streets, but also the typical image of the American commercial strip. Encourage students to lend their skills; both their knowledge and their practical help will add enjoyment to the process and contribute to your effort.

Explore Mutual Interests with Private Corporations

There are any number of private organizations (both profit and nonprofit) that may have their own reasons for supporting your project. Corporations, banks, major department stores, and private institutions may be of great assistance in promotional backing and actual funding, even though they may not be located along your street.

Some nonprofit organizations are good sources for volunteers. For instance, Phoenix House, a drug-prevention group in New York, supplied volunteers for the revitalization of West Seventy-third Street. On your street, volunteers may come from a neighborhood church or the PTA.

Corporations with business interests on your street should be explored as a financial resource. Branch banks, utility companies, and owners of major department stores will be receptive. Many have investments there in the form of large parcels of land and buildings. Also, they might have budget allocations for community projects.

A good-will program, along with community help, will improve the public image of large corporations. Each year, millions of dollars' worth of private funding is spent by large institutions that want to demonstrate their concern for neighborhoods. Furthermore, businesses, and most especially banks, will readily recognize the impact of revitalization on land values. After all, the role of a bank includes financing healthy businesses in its area, and lowering the risk of economic instability. If you can get the cooperation of a bank, it will become an incentive for other private investment to follow suit.

From the Bank of America in San Francisco to Citibank in New York City, large financial institutions are on record as public servants as well as custodians of cash and credit. And, in other areas of corporate life, the record is impressive. Johnson Wax, headquartered in Racine, Wisconsin, is known for having commissioned the great architect Frank Lloyd Wright to design its buildings; and more recently, the company has invested millions to upgrade the quality of Racine's downtown streets and open spaces. The John Deere Company, in Moline, Illinois, is recognized for its sensitivity to design; it commissioned such renowned architects as Eero Saarinen, Kevin Roche, and John Dinkeloo. For the local residents, the company is mainly known for having encouraged the renewal of an old business district and the beautification of the Rock River banks. In New York City, the long-planned improvements for Fourteenth Street and the adjacent Union Square district are now being implemented with financial aid from Consolidated Edison, the utility company, which is headquartered on that street.

Approaching a major corporation like DuPont or General Motors is different from soliciting the support of a small merchant along your street. Don't be afraid, while being tactful about it, to ask them for help in proportion to their means. Ask for what you need: You will soon discover that it's difficult to go back a second time.

Preservation Groups Are Good Allies

There are many other organizations, in the fields of art, cultural affairs, historic and architectural preservation, that would view your project as a prototype, using street revitalization to promote cultural activities in your community. If your street has a major landmark or a collection of distinctive buildings, the historic conservation groups will be eager to prove the benefits of renovating and reusing architecturally significant structures. You can depend on such groups for continued help because they have a vested interest in making sure that your street revitalization will not only enhance your street visually, but also preserve its historic quality. Saving older buildings protects the scale and the physical continuity

of your street and, at the same time, serves as a spiritual link between the present and the past. The preservation of Grand Central Terminal, a major landmark case, prompted the interest in the improvement of all of Forty-second Street.

While you can expect help from wide-ranging and various interests outside your neighborhood, the ability of your own community to follow through will determine the amount of help you get from outside groups. After all, it's your street and it's your responsibility to coordinate and direct the process throughout.

Grand Central Terminal, N.Y.C.

A mural of Old Church Street as drawn by concerned citizens on a New York City street

The Strand in Galveston, Texas

Pike Place Market, Seattle — Interior View

Pike Place Market, Seattle — Exterior View

THE PLANNING PROCESS

Now that you have marshaled the forces within your street and have stimulated enthusiasm from outside, you're prepared to develop a plan for your street. Your street is unique and may require variations on the process described. However, certain common elements are shared by all streets. They are part of a functioning street system and they are locked in place by a surrounding community.

But mostly, there is something going for each street, something special, that could be the central focus of a plan. It is this quality that you must set out to discover and strengthen. It could be an ethnic flavor, or the predominant style and scale of the architecture.

A waterfront street on the Gulf Coast is different from a California street of open markets. A Philadelphia street of proper town houses is nothing like a Las Vegas street of nightspots. Don't try to change the character of your street; look for the qualities that you like and build your plan around them.

The Strand in Galveston, Texas, on the Gulf Coast, has one character. This long, spacious stretch from the old days of shipping and mercantile activity is being recycled. Out of a gritty and forlorn state, Victorian warehouses are being transformed into a glorious array of restaurants, shops, galleries, and loft apartments. The older residential streets of Long Beach, California, have another kind of character, with homes nestled unpretentiously beside inlets, canals, and marinas.

In Seattle's Pike Place, the famous multilevel market spills onto the streets with fresh vegetables and brightly colored flowers. The street becomes a maze of experiences for the pedestrian — open, light, and inviting.

Nashville's character reflects its role as the home of country and western music. The refurbishing of the Grand Ole Opry has sparked additional improvements in the vicinity: among them a number of projected commercial buildings, surrounding a plaza called "The Plink," with storefronts featuring variations on this musical theme, where pedestrians will be able to peer into real-life recording studios.

The expression of character can vary widely, even when two different streets have the same width, length, and style of architecture. Similar building heights, a sympathetic range of color, texture, and materials — all bestow a sense of continuity. A street's character, however, derives from the people who live and work there — how they actually use it. In New York City, there are many beautiful, tree-lined brownstone streets. While they all appear similar at first glance, a closer look reveals their differences. There is a contrast between West 9th Street in Greenwich Village and East Sixty-second Street on the Upper East Side. On 9th Street, artists living in the first-floor apartments often hang their paintings in the streetside windows as a form of promotion. Building superintendents, residents, and passers-by chat on the street at all hours of the day, amid a friendly, cheerful atmosphere. These ad hoc galleries and the constant activity give the street diversity in contrast to the unified background of the street's architecture. On the other hand, the architectural unity of East Sixty-second Street is uninterrupted. The neighbors often don't know one another and prefer a more private, sedate sharing of urban impulses.

A street's character develops over time and, like a patina, cannot be formed overnight.

Look for the fundamental character of your own street with similar insight; consider the mix of people, activities, and buildings that make it special. Then set out to amplify that uniqueness.

East 62nd St. in New York City

Your Impact Area

The part of the city immediately around your street is your impact area. Your street's relationship to other streets and to the surrounding neighborhood is crucial. Every street in your city is a link to other streets. Be sure your process does not lead to a design concept that gives the feeling that you've left town when you get there.

Identifying the character of a street and knowing its people is only part of the task. Practical considerations are important as well. It is essential to consider questions of transportation, traffic and pedestrian circulation, street uses, all of which must then be integrated with the physical restoration plans while strengthening the street's character. A good place to begin is with the issue of accessibility. After all, to be a success, your street must be easy to get to.

Most streets have several points of arrival. Ask yourself where these are. From which adjacent streets, for example, do cars and pedestrians turn onto your street? What kinds of structures and activities are located at those intersections? How do the concentrations of cars or people change from hour to hour, day to day, and on weekends and holidays? Are there subway stations? Where are the gas stations located? Are there bus stops or taxi stations? Understand these practical aspects of your street in advance in order to grasp the problems in depth before you start specific improvements. To have a successful plan, you have to go through a great number of details — collecting information, organizing data, and analyzing it. This is where you really begin to assume command of the street-improvement process.

The First Step — Collecting Data: At this point you will have to spend a lot of time and energy collecting data. Just as legwork is behind every good newspaper story, research is behind every good revitalization project. You cannot solve your street's problems until you have identified and analyzed them. There is no definite point where data collection ends and analysis begins. You will instinctively start analyzing the moment you have made a mental note of what's there.

Collecting data cannot be restricted to your individual street. Visit the adjoining streets and adjacent neighborhoods, discern how functions invariably overlap, and analyze how conditions might affect your specific situation.

Do not leap to conclusions before you have all your data. Your first impression, for example, may be that people are not spending time on your street because the buildings are rundown. Look farther: They may not be coming because it is difficult to get to. Is there a tangle of trucks on a nearby thoroughfare slowing up traffic? Are public transit stops inundated with fumes or are the subway stations dismal? Must one walk from major parking areas, passing through dark vacant lots or passageways?

In the course of collecting this practical data, your sensibilities should be open to the pulse of the community. A surface look at certain areas would have deprived us of some favorite neighborhoods. Around the country, areas that were considered ''dead'' in the recent past have become major centers of rejuvenation and significant city sections. This is certainly true about San Francisco's waterfront, Seattle's Pioneer Square, Chicago's Navy Pier and old Printing House Row areas, and New York City's Soho. In Soho, residents and artists discovered the charm of old cast-iron buildings and realized that former warehouses could be revitalized and made marketable for new residential and retail uses. You, too, should look for those assets that, even if not obvious at first, can make the difference on your own street.

Get to Know your Neighborhood: Nearby streets and the adjoining neighborhoods provide important information to understanding your own street, whether the reference is to traffic patterns, the mix of economic activities, the physical layout of the blocks, or to architectural qualities and scale. Knowledge of this impact area is important because people enter and leave your street by way of its surroundings, and because any improvements that you make will influence those surroundings. Even a small change will have a ripple effect on your neighborhood. Similarly, a change that has been proposed on a nearby street, such as the construction of a high-rise building on a nearby residential block, will influence your plan. It could, for example, add many more

Pioneer Square, Seattle

shoppers on your street.

If your impact area has heavy traffic, big trucks, or a highway, your street's chances for success are impeded, and you will have to confront the problems of noise, fumes, and access. Two courses of action are possible. Ideally, you could induce the traffic department to change traffic-flow patterns in order to disperse congestion away from your street. A less ambitious approach would be to evaluate carefully your access areas and perhaps change them to connect with less busy streets. You want to minimize any adverse effects that the impact area has on your street. You don't want outside pressures to result in your street being used for purposes that impede the street's usefulness as a pleasant place for people to be.

On the other hand, you may find that in your impact area you have overlooked an opportunity that your street can offer to everyone's benefit. Perhaps there is a vacant lot that could be transformed into a playground, or a small park where workers might go to have lunch. There might be a partially occupied building on your street that could be reused as a center for community use or attractive shops. At this point, you may want to investigate the possibility of getting community development money for, perhaps, a day-care cen-

ter that might be located in such a building. Search out every possible connection between the available resources and the needs of your community. In New York City, for example, P.S. 1, an abandoned school building, was transformed into a modern art center that improved the whole neighborhood overnight.

Since your street is part of a functioning city street system and is locked in place by a surrounding community, studying your impact area is crucial to your project. It is critical for you to know the peripheral forces that may influence your immediate area and to find ways to minimize any environmental conflicts. Yet at the same time, you should be aware that your street may become a source of amenities that are lacking in the neighborhood. And finally, while your street improvement may be a small-scale undertaking, it is only the first stage toward a total neighborhood transformation.

Define Your Specific Impact Area: Where, within what boundaries, is your own impact area? How far it reaches beyond your street is something that collecting data will tell you, provided that you integrate and direct the information toward a realistic goal. Bear in mind, as you look out from your own street towards your impact area for information, that you must constantly cross-reference those facts and figures with those related to your specific improvements. Otherwise you'll be lost in a maze of irrelevant detail. Also remember that you are dealing with the kinds of goals and improvements that are possible, not the kinds that remain visions of utopia.

Just as you can't go on collecting data forever (piling up numbers and notes can be a form of evading real action), you can't go on forever defining an impact area. In looking to understand how your own street relates to and reflects the community around it, let the dominant physical, social, and natural facts of the setting be your guide as to where you draw the line.

Often a park, a river, a nearby cross street, or a highway will define the borders of the impact area. Or the borders of the area might be defined by a change in the style or scale of the buildings, or by the difference in use in the economic or industrial activity from block to block, as your street threads through the area.

For example, if you were to improve part of Sunset Boulevard, Los Angeles, a magnificent street which winds for miles through a variety of uses, from the university facilities of UCLA to the expensive Beverly Hills mansions to the renowned entertainment/commercial district known as "the strip," the question would be where would you draw the line in defining your impact area? The border of your study in such a case would be limited to the stretch of the street you want to improve, rather than to the entire length of the street. If the entertainment section of the street requires improvement, for instance, you will define its borders around that predominant use. But your impact area borders should encompass a larger area on both sides of the strip to include the neighborhoods directly affected by your improvement. You don't need to study all of Los Angeles, but consider the relationship between the specific street and its surrounding area. In the long run, your plan will have immediacy and importance that will reinforce improvements nearby. And while any positive action along your street will benefit the neighborhood, you cannot save everything at once.

Set realistic goals in determining your borders. After all, if you collect data on half of your town, you may never begin your own street project. There is a point where analysis must begin. Through the process, you may find that you need more information in one area or subject and have to go back to find more specific data. This effort will be worthwhile, since it will be directed toward a more defined goal. It is useful to break down the information into several categories; you may add some more depending on your situation.

• Circulation: Do people get to, or through, your street by car, mass transit, on bicycles, or on foot? How many in each mode of travel?

• Traffic: Check the volume of vehicles and pedestrians. Find the key generators of your traffic and the points of its major concentration; for example: subway stations, bus stops, drive-in fast-food outlets, parking lots, gas stations. Then analyze the traffic and pedestrian movement and directions from these sources to your street. Don't forget the trucks that service your stores.

• Uses of land: Study the buildings that line your street. Evaluate their architectural style and scale and determine their use. Are there cafes, grocery stores, and family residences? Are they high-rise or low-rise buildings? Do you have a church, park, or playground along your street? Where are these located, and what is their physical condition?

• Activities: Note the daytime and nighttime uses of your street. A part of your street that is dynamic at one time of the day may be deserted at another, or it may be bustling during the week and deserted on weekends. The activities at ground level will determine how people use your street's sidewalks. A department store will attract many more people than a bank, for instance. Remember that part of the pleasure of a place consists of the spontaneity of people gathering, for different occasions, at many times during the day. Note what people are doing, either along your street or inside the buildings. Record everything, from groups of people conversing on front stoops to those lining up to see a movie.

• Character: Does your street have a cultural,

The street as a playground, Bronx, N.Y.C

12

ethnic, aesthetic, and historical uniqueness? The sources of character are legion. Look for the physical elements that make your street different. It may be the architectural detailing or the colors people paint their windowsills. Look for any signals. Sometimes the street's essence is derived from an ethnic base. Identify the makeup of your community. Is it a residential street in Knoxville, Tennessee, where people sit peacefully rocking on their porches watching traffic pass by, or is it a shopping street in the North End of Boston with pasta and sausage displayed in the storefronts?

Interpreting the Data: No matter what may seem obvious or apparent from your data, always make data analysis a separate process from data collection. First, draw up maps (all in the same scale) that present visually each of the categories described. These maps will provide you with a clear, in-depth understanding of the issues involved. Then, superimpose the information maps, one on top of the other, and begin to analyze the relationship of one function to another. This will help you to see what already exists, and thereby envision improvement possibilities with greater accuracy and realism. You can now approach the raw data from several vantage points and you will comprehend the interrelationships of the physical elements on the street, both those that are compatible with your goal and those that are sources of conflict.

When you overlay a map showing the condition of buildings over your land-use map, you may find a vacant building that happens to be a landmark. Your hardware map — showing the placement of fire hydrants, emergency lanes, and delivery entrances — superimposed over your pedestrian map will give you an accurate estimate of how much room remains for additional amenities such as benches and trees.

Superimposing a map showing traffic volume over a map showing pedestrian circulation will immediately point up problem areas. You may want to add more room for pedestrians. Go back and reexamine your impact area traffic map, and evaluate whether you can give up a traffic lane for a widened sidewalk and redirect vehicles to a parallel street. These maps are the key tools for a comprehensive understanding of your street.

A crowded subway entrance, N.Y.C.

Circulation and Accessibility: Your street won't be a success if people can't get there. Access has to be not only easy, but inviting as well. Contact city hall or the right agency for maps that will help you to understand points of access, as well as the more technical traffic maps that show the volume and direction of traffic. These will help you prepare your own information maps. In asking for them, be sure the maps are up to date. (A traffic map made before a new shopping mall was built is inaccurate.) Sometimes the agency will help you update the maps; otherwise you will have to do this yourself.

In many cities, the bus, train, or subway may be the easiest way for outsiders to get to a street. A subway or bus stop may be the origin of pedestrian movement, i.e., people on their way to work, going home, or arriving from some other part of town for an evening. In other cities, the best access to a street may be by car. Since your goal is to encourage the pedestrian to come and enjoy your street the placement of convenient parking lots becomes important. Making access to your street easy and pleasant is as important a task. Heavy traffic in the immediate area or on your own street may turn visitors away. Make note of when the traffic is heaviest, comparing rush hours to nonrush hours, and check the volume at night and on weekends. The state of a street can change quite quickly: what is charming

Traffic jam in Manhattan

over a weekend, when truck traffic is absent from the area, can be horrendous the rest of the week.

You will notice that a retail street gets most of its traffic during the day and that a streetful of cafes and other night spots comes alive in the evening. A street with architectural or historical appeal or one with a potpourri of specialty shops, antique dealers, or art galleries will get most of its visitors on weekends. Knowing when your street is most active will enable you to concentrate on pertinent traffic problems.

If heavy traffic is your problem, and if relieving some of it seems justified by your project, it may be possible to reroute the traffic to nearby streets that can handle more cars. Perhaps half of a street's traffic can be eliminated by simply making the street one-way. It would be advisable to work with your highway department at an early stage in order to avoid later complications. Make sure that you do not create a problem in the process of solving one. Closing one street can change the traffic patterns in your town.

The Pedestrian Right-of-Way: Your challenge is to turn a motorist into a pedestrian as soon as possible. Scout the general area for parking lots or garages that are within walking distance of your street. You may find streets that have heavy traffic during business hours but are empty in the evening and on weekends. If evening and weekend activities are what you are trying to

build up, these streets will often provide the parking spaces you need. But if the parking that is available is used most of the time by the residents of the area, you will have to find additional parking facilities.

Once visitors are converted to pedestrians, there is the question of how far they are willing to walk. This varies from city to city. In Los Angeles, the private car is practically a biological extension; even a five-minute walk is considered long. The same is true of Phoenix, Houston, and other Sun Belt cities. But in cities with some pedestrian network, a general rule of thumb is that people will walk six to ten minutes before they hop on a bus, dive into a subway, or hail a cab. One truth transcends all rules: people will walk longer if the walk is particularly pleasant or stimulating. There is a direct relationship between the sun, views, and activity and general appeal along the street and the distance people are willing to walk. People will walk forever on San Francisco's Union Street, New York's Fifth Avenue, or New Orleans' Bourbon Street. In Manhattan, crowds roam from Little Italy to Soho, the famous artists' haven, to Orchard Street and Chinatown. When walking is fun, the time doesn't matter. A good walk to get to your street can be a pleasure as well as a necessity.

In your own study, figure out the radius around your own street that includes a walking distance of six to ten minutes. See what transit stops and

Walking is fun along Fifth Avenue, N.Y.C.

parking facilities are within this area and determine whether the most direct walk from public transportation to your street is a pleasant one. The route may be livened up with more lighting or landscaping. And adding stores if more are needed always increases pedestrian interest.

The ambiance of your street is derived from its shops, its architecture and scale, its landscaping and from its people and their activities within the buildings. To grasp the essence of your place you must become familiar with the concept referred to by planners as land-use, which describes many of these properties.

Land-use and Zoning Maps: Zoning and land-use maps will show the scale and configuration of buildings and how the land is used. Are the buildings residential, commercial, or manufacturing? Where is the major shopping center located? The zoning maps will also indicate the volume of building allowed and the density of residents in the area. Get the land-use maps for your impact area from the appropriate city agency. You may be lucky and find detailed land-use maps that will show parking spaces and vacant lots and maybe even the condition of buildings. Be sure these maps are as up to date as possible. Such current information will help you to know the exact, present state of the buildings you will be dealing with — and where new vacant land is available. Not many cities are as fortunate in this respect as Eugene, Oregon, which routinely updates its maps by computer.

After consulting these maps, go over and look at these areas in person to verify their accuracy (you may need to update them) and to discover new opportunities that your impact area may provide. Also look for what the impact area lacks; perhaps you can make up for such deficiencies as part of your project. Maybe open space is unavailable. When none exists nearby, an improved vacant lot could become a place for sitting in the sun, a playground, or a plaza luring shoppers.

Finally, the architectural, historic, or geographical assets of the area might well suggest your street as a primary pedestrian link to such places of interest. Los Angeles' Olvera Street, for instance, makes a fine walk between historic Union

Olvera Street, Los Angeles

Station and Chinatown. Always remember that you are looking for something special, either what is inherent in your street or sources in the vicinity that your street can connect with.

Your Own Street

Now that you are familiar with your neighborhood through data collection and analysis, you are well prepared to focus on your immediate goal: your own street.

You are not alone, by any means, in your resolve to better your neighborhood. Increasingly, as you look around the country, this kind of perspective and impulse is taking hold as street organizations and neighborhood groups become more sophisticated and effective in municipal planning, politics, and in establishing development corporations. From Seattle to Savannah, the policies that deal with the development of streets, districts, and neighborhoods are stressing the maintenance of important views and the adaptive reuse of existing structures. Also appearing with increasing force are design guidelines regarding the height, bulk, materials, textures, and the range of colors to be used in new construction, thus better ensuring a sympathetic tie between new and old. San Francisco, Minneapolis, Cincinnati, Baltimore, Boston, Boulder (Colorado), Salem (Massachusetts), and many other cities, have innovative criteria in force. These are precedents you can cite, and tools you can use, as you begin the process on your own turf and terms.

If this process of collection and analysis seems dry and tedious at times, you must not forget that you are acting upon the very real feelings of people. What you do with your data must constantly reconcile objective information with a sensitive approach. Always keep in mind what people really want: a street where people recognize a familiar face, a place to sit and read a book, a place for the children to play, a meeting place to chat with friends, a vibrant, diverse street, full of attractively displayed merchandise where they can spend their time and money, never feeling that either was wasted. These desires are hard to measure, but a street revitalization project that ignores them will miss the reason for getting involved in this challenge in the first place.

The emphasis on data should not be interpreted as a dispassionate practice, devoid of basic concern for improving people's outlook. As the great architect Louis Kahn once said, "A city is a place where a small boy, as he walks through it, can see something that will tell him what he wants to do his whole life." If your street does not now have that kind of human resonance, with the right responsive attitude it can in the future.

The Street as a Room: Zooming in on your own street, being familiar with its larger surroundings, you are ready to get to know your street intimately. Every city street is a three-dimensional space. Think of your street as a room. The road and the sidewalks are your floor. The facades and elevations of the buildings are your walls. The sky framed through the buildings is your ceiling.

This outdoor room has a certain range of architectural detail, a variety of uses, and numerous people who live or work there. Look behind the walls and see how people use the spaces inside and how these uses relate to your street.

As in your impact area study, you want to understand the logistics and functions of your street. Again, gather your data and make your maps: vehicular entrances and exits; traffic patterns and volume; pedestrian circulation; servicing patterns; hardware location; mass transit stops and parking lots. All should be gathered in great detail.

Beyond the logistics is a larger question. Just

what is it in this "room" you are here to improve? What is unique? What is its character? After all, a successful design concept can only come from the strength that is already there and the energy and creativity you bring to the revitalization process.

First Impressions: Character, like personality, is too elusive to define in a way that would apply to every street in any city. But there are specifics you can look for. Architecture is one. Historical character is another. Or you could study the retail activity that makes the street so personal and civilized — outdoor cafes, night spots, bookstores, waterfront-related activities, or open markets.

Sometimes what a street is near gives it an identity. A street near a park, a university, a stadium, or a beach will adopt the unique character of its surroundings and be a multifaceted profile of its residents as well.

Mulberry Street, in Little Italy, has its Italian spirit. In Santa Barbara, California, the Spanish arcades and roofs of tile give State Street its graceful air and unity.

Portland, Maine, has a unique New England mix of salty, simple brick and stone structures, with decorative details at entrances and on windowsills. The close-grained network of streets thread down to the waterfront, and from either end of them tight, vivid, unexpected perspectives open up.

The streets of Lowell, Massachusetts, derive

State Street, Santa Barbara

Vieux Carré, New Orleans
View from a rooftop

Vieux Carré, New Orleans
Detail of a street corner

much of their character from the old textile mills and canals. They depict elements of the Industrial Revolution, as much as a sturdy, no-nonsense 19th-century architectural style. The canals originally serving the textile industry have been cleaned, and recreational leisure paths aligning both sides now meander through the city. Lowell is now America's first Urban National Park.

Bourbon Street in New Orleans (named for the French royal dynasty, not the beverage) is known as much for its music, nightlife, and parades as for its cast-iron balconies. In fact, the building elements are subsumed in all the socializing. Everything, from the blues to the architecture, is integral to the street's ambiance, which filters from the street itself back into many intimate courts.

Sometimes, people's way of life distinguishes one community from another. Find out who lives along your street. Is there a predominant ethnic group: Italian, Spanish, Greek, Chinese, German, Polish, or a mix? Is it Greek in spirit like Tarpon Springs, Florida, or Chinese in spirit like San Francisco's Chinatown? And even though your street, like most streets, may not have an apparent ethnic flavor, its still important to understand the lives, origins, and general values of the people who live there. Harvard Square in Cambridge, Massachusetts, for instance, owes most of its character, particularly on Brattle Street, to Har-

vard University and the many nearby academic institutions.

Your plan should reflect the particular needs and habits of the people living along your street. A neighborhood that has many elderly people may require extra seating space, while an area with large families may need a new playground for children.

There is nothing like meeting the people on your street to discover what is in fact going on. Talk to the merchants, your baker, or meet the manager of the nearest savings bank. These people have a good idea of who their customers are and where they come from. These insights and impressions go beyond the mere collecting of cold facts. You are learning the nature of your street by acquiring a greater understanding of its people. As Frank Lloyd Wright once said, "Human nature is the primary building material."

Pedestrian Patterns: Pedestrian movement along your street is influenced by the kind of shops found there, the number of residents, and even the pattern of delivery of goods and services.

There are three ways that pedestrians use a street. They shop, they stroll, or they use it as a route to get from one place to the other (from home to the subway, for instance). From your study of the neighboring impact area, you already know the visitors' points of entrance and their possible destinations. Now you want to find out how they use the street once they actually get there.

Take particular note of the number of-people and where they congregate on the street, as well as where they are likely to encounter obstacles. This knowledge is important because you want to turn as many visitors as possible into pedestrians, and to do that you'll have to minimize any conflicts on their way.

A conflict is anything that makes being a pedestrian difficult or unpleasant. It could be crowds lining up outside a movie theater or waiting to get into a bus at rush hours, making it difficult for passers-by. It could be heavy traffic or a lack of crosswalks or signal lights. It might be something as simple as gashes in the sidewalk or discarded cardboard boxes stacked up outside a supermarket.

You learn about pedestrian movement by observation, and you should be as thorough as possible here, noting the numbers of pedestrians, their behavior, and the elbow room the sidewalk permits. You want to know the street by day and the street by night. You'll want to find out when different kinds of enterprises have their peak periods of use — bowling alleys, restaurants, theaters, schools, and churches.

The amount of information you need will depend on the scope of the problem. For example, on Mulberry Street, storefronts were recorded according to location, type of business, and the intensity of traffic they generated; it was found that the restaurants and pastry shops drew the biggest crowds during the evenings and on weekends. How do you get these pedestrian counts if you want to be more accurate? You might go out (or get students to help) and count people at peak hours. For larger, more dense areas with more complex pedestrian traffic patterns, the use of time-lapse photography is becoming a popular method, as was done in Midtown Manhattan, where the Regional Plan Association of New York photographed pedestrians and related their destinations to the uses of the street, establishing which activities attracted the highest volume. This method is costly and is only suitable for vast metropolitan areas. In the majority of cases, and

most likely for your street, the simpler tactic of standing with a stopwatch at peak hours on a congested spot, regularly recording the number of people or just making careful notes, will serve your purpose.

You will notice that while some places attract people, other places deter them. Blank walls, vacant sites, parking lots, factories, abandoned buildings break up the street's retail continuity. Along Mulberry Street, where the shops are often interrupted by factories at ground level, such locations were recorded precisely. In the final plan the community used these same locations on weekends, when the factories were closed, for artistic or recreational events. A weekend art show can make even a blank brick wall seem friendly.

Sidewalks are for People: The major emphasis on the convenience of the auto is a trend that is barely fifty years old and already suspect. Think of your street as a place to attract and engage others, a place where walking is preferable to being behind the wheel. Your street is a place for shopping, sitting, kissing, walking dogs, and making friends. The nicer you make your street for strolling, the more strollers you'll get.

Making the street visually attractive is not enough. You want to find the newsstand that is popular in the morning, an ice cream parlor that gets most of its business from the noontime crowds, a fountain around which couples gather. Familiarize yourself with these areas as you plan for your pedestrian environment. The quality of the merchandise and an imaginative window display will attract new shoppers from even distant places. Any action to help your merchants make their signage and their displays elegant and inviting will improve your street's image and increase their clientele.

Finally, people simply love to watch other people. People will stand on the corner watching the parade go by, but sometimes a bench is desirable. As William H. Whyte has pleaded, "*Please*, just a place to sit!"

Provide more places for people to sit, on benches or at sidewalk cafes, and make sure you leave room for those passers-by who are in a hurry. The pedestrian who simply wants to get from one place to another — from a bus to work, from a parking lot to a movie — can think of your street either as a barrier course or as the one bright spot in his travels. Sidewalk size and comfort will influence his course. Since streets are supposed to be routes as well as destinations, you owe the runners the same consideration as the walkers.

Studying the width and capacity of your sidewalks, relative to where pedestrians concentrate, is important. The main point is to ensure sufficient space so that the street, and its sidewalks, can handle the different activities that customarily occur — along with the new ones you are proposing.

The sidewalk space that presently exists may not be all that you can offer the pedestrian. Sometimes it is possible, after having studied traffic volume and determining that some traffic can be redirected to other streets, to convert one lane to allow more space for strollers. Borrowing such a lane would naturally make pedestrian circulation easier around cafes or in front of shops where people queue up. You might even consider dividing one lane into two areas, partly to add sidewalk room and partly to form paths for bicycles. This is a way to reduce your traffic, allowing more room for people on foot, and even to make your street more popular to cyclists, a growing minority. In all cases, ease of access and movement for the physically disabled is not only a matter of decency but also a legal requirement. Be sure to work this consideration into your planning for sidewalk improvements.

Sidewalk cafe impedes the pedestrian
Third Ave., New York City

What Moves, What Doesn't: There is a strong interrelationship between the things along your street that move and those objects that are stationary — for example, the relationship of the fire hydrant to the fire engine, the utility companies to the power lines, the delivery trucks to the loading docks, even the automobile to the curb. Cars, mass transit, commercial and residential servicing, and the pedestrian all influence each other. These relationships may be smooth or strained. But you'll have to know just how the relationships work in order to see what can be done, and determine the long-range consequences of your action. You will identify two kinds of conflicts: between pedestrians and traffic, and pedestrians and hardware.

Every seat is taken in a New York City Plaza

Parking Along the Street: It is quite likely that people will arrive at your street by car. Since you want to improve the access to your street as well as the pedestrian environment, you will want to find every opportunity to get people out of their cars and onto your street in a comfortable and pleasant way.

In planning for a better integration of traffic and parking within a convenient pedestrian surrounding, the following key issues should be considered:
● how to limit conflict areas between cars and the pedestrian;
● what is the appropriate size and location of

parking facilities;
● how to relate visually the parking areas to the rest of your street.

Everyone has experienced at least once the feeling of chaos along a street where the car competes with, and overwhelms, the pedestrian. This confusion can be eliminated if the areas where the car belongs and where the pedestrian right-of-way is located are clearly marked. The intent here, after all, is to establish an environment where people can walk freely and undisturbed, a place that imparts a sense of order and safety as people stroll along the street or as they get from their parked cars to their shopping destinations.

Simple indicators, such as a change in paving material or use of color, can delineate bus lanes or pedestrian crossings. The placement of attractive ballards can define the periphery of parking areas. These are only two ways to differentiate between traffic lanes and pedestrian right-of-ways.

Investigate with your traffic department ways of simplifying your traffic patterns and making them move more smoothly. Traffic concentrations that create congestion and pollution should be avoided. These annoyances are common around parking facilities and in areas where alternate side of the street parking is used. Alternate side of the street parking often causes double-parking, a critical problem for both the traffic and the pedestrian. Now that you have given the visitor a reason to linger on your street and have, ideally, provided a central parking facility nearby, you may get rid of the half-hour parking meters that result in a large turnover of cars pulling out of parking spaces every 30 minutes.

The amount of parking space that you will need varies from place to place. In areas without a mass transit system, you will obviously require more parking areas, and therefore you will have to create additional spaces. This may call for the acquisition of new land for parking which may entail a substantial public or private investment. However, there may be an inherent incentive for both the city and the private developer to add parking to your street. City-sponsored parking sometimes brings revenue to the city, while privately owned parking areas are often profitable.

In fact, we are all too familiar with cases where communities and private interests confront each other over the demolition of a noteworthy building destined to be replaced by an open parking lot.

Often you will find that the potential for additional parking already exists on your street and that the creation of new facilities do not always mean a major investment. Scout around for adequate space. You may want to recycle vacant lots or rearrange parking meters. Be ingenious in finding the space you need. Increase your parking at night and on weekends by allowing parking in areas that are normally used for trucking and business-related services during working hours. Also, study the plans of any new development to see if you can negotiate with the private developer to include new parking floors in his building.

Providing more parking is one challenge. Reducing the size of huge parking areas, which, like missing teeth, interrupt the life and line of your street, is another. Whether you need more parking or are blessed with plenty of spaces, it is essential that you locate your parking along the periphery of your street so that parking is convenient and easily accessible, while, at the same time, parked cars do not interrupt the flow of traffic. You may not have the option of redirecting your traffic or locating your parking lots on adjacent blocks around your street, or even of tucking your parking out of sight. But make sure that you have studied all the opportunities for your parking plan within your impact area. Identify the location and sizes of existing parking lots, as well as the direction of the traffic, placing emphasis on entrances and exits as they converge with any pedestrian activity.

Once you have decided the appropriate location and size of your parking area and resolved the conflicts between the car and the pedestrian, you want to insure that your parking facilities are as attractive as possible. If a new garage is constructed along your street, persuade the owner to provide retail or community facilities at ground level. It is much more pleasant and enticing to walk by an ice cream parlor than by a row of parked cars. If this is not possible, maybe a colorful mural along the facade can make the garage seem more friendly. Be creative in finding ways to buffer large parking areas from your street. You may be lucky and convince a parking lot

S.I.T.E. sculpture buffers parking lot
Hamden, Connecticut

owner to "contribute" twenty feet in front for retail activities, for landscaping, or as a location for a work of environmental art. "Site," an environmental artist group, has cast cars in concrete along a parking lot in Hamden, Connecticut, adding humor and beauty to the streetscape. Don't forget to provide adequate lighting. In areas with severe winters, a covered passageway from the parking facilities to your street may be desirable.

Despite the trend in this country, as a result of the energy crisis, to produce smaller cars, and a renewed interest in mass transit, it is apparent that the car will remain a major consideration in your approach. In some parts of the country, watching cars driving on Main Street is still a popular sport. Recognize the phenomenon of the car and deal with it in the right perspective. After all, the street's revitalization, its cultural ambiance, the quality of the air, and the level of noise will be affected by how well you address parking and traffic problems.

Hardware and Servicing: There are a variety of objects which are fixed into the bed of your sidewalk, such as utility poles, parking meters, mailboxes, gradings, telephone booths, and other street furniture. It is important to include these objects, called hardware in planner's language, in the plan for your street. Assume that a major light pole is located just at the area that you envision as a sitting area, for instance; or that a row of telephone booths is located so as to impede the flow of pedestrian traffic. Your first reaction would be to remove or relocate such fixed objects. But to avoid delays and extra expense, it would be best to examine carefully which of these objects can be relocated easily and which ones would entail going through a lengthy bureaucratic procedure. The simplest way, of course, would be to develop your plan around the existing hardware. After all, you don't want to make a federal case out of moving a mailbox.

Another practical issue, which needs your concern at an early stage, is the complex networks of custodians that service both streets and buildings.

For the most part, you will be concerned with utility, commercial and emergency services — both municipal and private. The removal of snow, the pruning of trees, the maintenance, repair, and replacement of traffic signs, and garbage collection are usually municipal responsibilities. On the other hand, commercial servicing is generally done through private firms who regularly deliver stock to stores and provide services to offices and industries. Some cities, such as San Francisco, use private firms to collect garbage. Don't forget the utility services — the men and trucks who maintain water, gas, and electric lines. Finally, there are the emergency services, which include fire trucks, police cars, and ambulances, that must have access to your street at all times.

You will have to consider the unique procedures that each one of these services follows. Street cleaning and garbage collection are usually done on a schedule. Familiarize yourself with these timetables if you plan to close off your street to traffic. A shift of working schedules means overtime labor costs and may require you to supplement the city's normal services. Your Department of Parks, Public Works, Streets or Traffic may be able to supply this information.

Any plan for a retail street will have to include a careful analysis of commercial servicing. The scheduling, the type of vehicle used, and the buildings' service entrances vary from establishment to establishment. Many stores are serviced through special stairs leading to their basement and opening directly onto the sidewalk. Since these considerations affect all movement along your street, you should investigate ways to coor dinate service deliveries during off-hours, leaving the sidewalk relatively free during peak times of pedestrian use.

Servicing of utilities is another matter. It is amazing how rarely maps depicting all underground lines and other utilities are available in one place, but you will have to know the utilities' exact location. Modification of a street and sidewalk must not interfere with water, gas, power, and communication lines below. Similarly, any change in your underground utility will have an impact on the paving above. Access of repairmen to these lines and replacement of material should be considered. New lighting fixtures should not intrude on gas mains below, and new trees cannot be allowed to sink their roots into existing power lines. Aboveground utilities will affect your street visually; you don't want scattered telephone poles to obstruct a panoramic view. Thus, it is important that your hardware map includes both underground and aboveground utility equipment.

Emergency services inevitably assume priority. Any plan you have for intensifying pedestrian use or for closing the street to traffic should allocate room for emergency vehicles at all times. A free lane, varying in size from city to city, is required to allow for the maneuvering of emergency equipment. Your fire and police departments can give you data about access requirements and about the location of hydrants, extinguishers, and fire escapes. The more you know about prevention of emergencies, the fewer sirens you'll hear.

These analyses of your hardware and the servicing of your street will be a solid base for minimizing the conflicts along your street and for gauging realistically the opportunities that your street presents.

The Walls of the Street: Each street has its distinct architecture and scale, its own shops, homes, and open spaces. The visual character of your street, as defined by the materials, colors, texture, physical condition, and architectural quality, is revealed through the street walls. These walls or street elevations, are first to impress a neighborhood visitor. They frame the street's space and express the diversity of activities that go on behind them—through a window or a glass wall, you discover the story behind the walls. You can get immersed in an eye-catching sign, get a glimpse through an open door, or look up onto a balcony.

First, familiarize yourself with your street elevations in detail. Unfortunately, elevation drawings of the city's buildings and streets are seldom available except in landmark areas. It is quite an undertaking to prepare such drawings of your own street, since it involves photographing each building and drawing elevations in scale directly from the photos.

This was done in New York City for Mulberry Street, Newkirk Plaza, and Beach 20th Street. Each building was photographed, then elevations were drawn in scale along the full length of the street. First, a line marking the height of the building was drawn, then the windows, entrances, balconies, canopies, signs, fire escapes, and even decorative details of the facades were recorded.

What this technique did in New York, and what it will do for you, is to give the community a comprehensive look at their "room" as they had never really seen before. And this presentation in New York did something else. It gave the planners an opportunity to study, close-up, the conditions of the wall surfaces. Many of the walls have since either been cleaned or have had murals painted on them.

These "new views" of the elevations gave everybody a clearer image of the continuity of the buildings lining the sidewalks on either side of the street. Sometimes cutaway drawings of the streets and the buildings bordering them are needed—drawings that design professionals call "sections"—to see the relationship between the space in the buildings, the depth of buildings, the rear yards, the street, and any underground transit or utility lines.

In Newkirk Plaza, these "sections" — done just as though you had X-rayed the whole complex to reveal its insides — showed the relationship of the subway, the pedestrian level, the buildings lining that level, and service entrances. Sections are helpful when an underground or aboveground system such as a subway station or a major parking lot relates to your street, or when the elevations do not express what happens behind the walls — for example, in a situation where a small door leads to a theater that seats 3,000 people.

Elevations are tools for studying and recording locations and types of materials. For instance, if your street is rich with a variety of materials such as brick, stone, wood, concrete, steel, glass, then work out a simple grading system to describe the differences in the materials and their physical condition. Do the buildings need to be restored, painted, or cleaned? Use some symbol or code to simplify your work. Include trees and any other landscaping in these elevations, as well as all the details that the pedestrian actually sees at ground level and above. Study architectural elements such as cornice lines, reliefs, and awnings.

These details may later give you the clue to your entire design concept. Further, it will give you a comprehensive vision of the street as it is experienced. This will demonstrate how your street is first perceived — say as one comes up out of a subway, or gets off a bus, or drives in. What do these first impressions, these initial views, consist of? Show it graphically. Is the perspective of the street inviting, intriguing, and seemingly unified? Is the perspective blocked by some signs and made jarring and irregular by urban blight? Careful study of these elevations, sections, and photographs will give you a vivid idea of what it is like for *others* to walk into your street, along it, and out — and as vivid an idea of what steps can be taken to make these views, sensory "gateways" in effect, more pleasing.

In addition to your elevations, certain photographs will be useful — the view as you enter the street, be it from the bus stop or a parking lot, may be important. Photographs will also assist you in visualizing unique views along your street, such as a waterfront at the foot of a hill or the view of the White House from Pennsylvania Av-

enue. Whether these views are modest or grand, the point is that you should record them to get a sense of how the street is seen from different vantage points.

Signs Along the Facades: The first function of a sign is to be seen. Unfortunately, competition being what it is, the second function of a sign is to be seen more easily than other signs. This obsession to out-advertise other shops on the street may create one big eyesore for the visitor.

The signs on your street are a dominant part of the elevations. A visitor, in fact, is doomed to see a big *Tuxedos for Sale or Rent* before he is going to notice the once-elegant brownstone that the sign is on. Like the car, signs are a major part of the American landscape. Therefore, when you develop your street, you must find a way to integrate signs so that they add to your street and become an aesthetic contribution rather than a pollutant.

Signs reflect street character
Queens, New York City

Some of the most obvious problems with signs are that they are too often poorly designed, they tend to cover significant architectural details of buildings, and they cause visual chaos by introducing unharmonious sizes, colors, and lettering styles. Occasionally, such different sizes and colors may be the appropriate solution. In Las Vegas and on Broadway in New York City, the bigger and brighter the better. After all, visitors are there for excitement, and the excitement starts with the signs.

Your approach to signage should be governed

by the character of the street itself. If the street has an architectural character worth preserving, the signs should reflect this. This can be done by expressing the period in the graphic style of the signs, or by reducing the sign to a minimal size so as not to compete with the architecture. Santa Barbara does not allow signs that cover the city's Spanish architecture. In Old San Diego, the community controls signs in a downtown landmark district by insisting that graphics and lettering be of a pre-1870 vintage to complement the historic Spanish-American theme.

Hand-painted signs on glass, like the italic script on shop windows in Little Italy and the oriental flair of signs in Chinatown, help the visitor know that he has arrived. Whether the signs on your street are intended for people in cars or on foot will determine their appropriate scale and size. Often, street signage will require two scales —one for the driver and one for the pedestrian. The large signs are designed for drivers to comprehend from a distance within seconds. The big bold signs on California's Sunset Boulevard were designed to attract and entertain motorists, whereas signs for pedestrians are located at a height that is easy to read.

While you may want your signs to be elegant, polite, and engaging, you may still want to allow a variety of color, graphic styles, and logos. Designing a sign that relates to the unique historical character of a building or district is a major concern, but so is the matter of working out a signage program that allows for flexibility of individual expression when appropriate.

In Vail, Colorado, the coloration and even the materials of the signs are controlled to reflect a sort of "Swiss Village" character. In Corning, New York, the old main street has been skillfully revitalized with signs that are highly individualistic from building to building but which, because of consistent care in the quality of design and the similarity of scale, give the street a distinctly cohesive quality.

The most important thing to remember is that while signs can be chaotic in effect, as on a typical commercial strip where fast-food and hotel chains dominate, the use of signs can be a simple way to distinguish and present your street as an inviting place to do business or to just have fun.

Tony Rosenthal sculpture, N.Y.C.

Artwork—An Important Dimension: Works of art will add an important dimension to your street revitalization project, and will bring joy to your residents and visitors alike. You will find the artists a responsive group to your cause. They will envision the street as a challenging stage for creative and innovative ideas. Using art as part of the process can both change the existing environment as well as create a new one. A dramatic piece of sculpture, in a plaza on New York's East Side, was conceived by the artist Tony Rosenthal, who designed it as a total environment. The sculpture itself becomes the sitting and leisure area for the surrounding neighborhood, adding color and a human scale to an otherwise uneventful streetscape.

Sculpture can also be used to create a "sense of place." A place where people meet their friends, like the traditional bell tower in old medieval towns. This was the case in the design of the Louise Nevelson Park, a small but impressive triangular park in Lower Manhattan. The renowned sculptress integrated her "metal treelike" sculptures with actual trees, seating, and benches, transforming the open space into a small oasis amid high-rise office buildings.

The use of murals is a simple and most effective way to cover surfaces on blank walls and to include your community in the process of making art. The "Beautiful walls for Baltimore" and the "Public Art Fund Incorporated" program in New York are only two examples of programs that are successful in converting ordinary buildings into canvases of color. Both these programs are being supported by the state and federal governments, and as they improve the visual aspect of streets, they also provide employment for unemployed artists through the CETA program and other public employment agencies. Government support for artists in such programs is based upon the conviction that the creative process could bring the community and individual artists together. Thus, as part of these programs, all artwork, its style and design content, is brought to the community for review.

Good works of art in the appropriate environment can act not only as a major uplift to your street's visual image, but can also center attention on your street's and city's physical assets and sparkle and provoke the interest of different groups in your city.

This is what happened in 1979, in New York City, with "Celebration: New York in Color,"

Louise Nevelson Park, N.Y.C.

an exhibition of color photography, by 50 of the greatest photographers in the field, that was installed in every window up and down fashionable Fifth Avenue.

The idea, and the fact that great talent donated their work to the city in turn got the governor of the State of New York, the Fifth Avenue Association, the Association for a Better New York, and more than a hundred volunteers involved. Moreover, it got the cooperation and participation of eighty merchants along the street and, most important, the sponsorship of Warner Communications, Inc., who paid for the printing of the costly large prints and a festive opening event.

Pedestrians walking down the Avenue were dazzled by the beauty of the photographs and the creative integration of the merchandise with the artwork. And while the photographs were highly personal interpretations of the individual artists, the show inspired thousands to reflect in their own way on the jumping, jubilant physical qualities of the city.

Projects such as these do not have to be limited to the Fifth Avenues of this country. In your own saving process the Fifth Avenue experience applies as well. Although you may have limited access to getting major artists to contribute work, look for talent among your local artists, or else seek chidren's drawings. Your revitalization theme could be an exciting project for children of all ages to capture.

Also, remember that a variety of public and semipublic agencies are supporting the arts quite aggressively. The National Endowment for the Arts and Humanities, the America the Beautiful Fund, and your own State Council for the Arts are some programs to consider. Do not hesitate to approach private sources. Some private foundations or individuals would rather donate a work of art than get involved in the general funding of rehabilitating a street. Find out also if your own state or city requires a percentage of all new construction costs to be set aside for artwork.

It is important to remember as you approach your planning process that including works of art, and getting the artists involved, should be integrated in your project at the earliest stage of your journey.

The ethnic ambiance of Mulberry St., N.Y.C., defines its theme and character.

DISCOVERING A THEME FOR YOUR STREET

A strong visual theme threading through your street will set it apart from other streets. The word "theme" here has much the same meaning as it has in music. It ties all the street elements together so that you get a definite impression of the street as you see it.

Mozart, a master at establishing and making variations on a theme, realized that the very force and cohesion of a theme could be heightened by interfacing highly contrasting elements now and again. The unexpected, carefully worked into a larger framework, can make the overall theme more dynamic.

Recognize those variations that add accents to the total image of your street. Its uniqueness can be generated from a variety of sources, ranging from the ethnic flavor and the mix of stores to the architectural style of the buildings and will make the difference between whether the street is looked upon as an avenue or an alley. Look at the way your street is used — for festivals, fairs, or just for a quiet stroll. Any unique signs and graphics? How is the merchandise displayed? Some of the most effective street uses are spontaneous attractions. In New York, practically overnight, Korean fruit-and-vegetable stores began sprouting up in older buildings breaking the physical monotony of the tall buildings above, adding color and a different rhythm. Look for the features that contribute to your street's authentic environment. Once

Rich architecture and a mix of stores give Quincy Market, Boston, its unique character.

Orchard St. in New York City

your street's theme becomes apparent, *it* should become the source of your ideas.

Too often designers have failed to recognize those existing qualities; rather than reinforce them, they impose their own tastes. Others are carried away by fashionable, trendy designs. Also beware of the designer's temptation for "the clean approach." Controlling the signs, getting rid of the peddlers and vendors, cleaning everything up may sap the existing vitality which you are attempting to preserve. It is often easier to control signage or to remove street peddlers than to integrate them in the new design. Eliminating billboards in the Times Square area would leave it stripped of its essence. The ad hoc quality of the neon signs and the marquees are part of the streets' theatrical theme, and should inspire the designer to integrate the billboards and neon into any new concept to improve the street's appearance.

In a similar spirit, but in a contrasting context, the improvement of the Washington Avenue area in Old Miami Beach, a mile-square of Art Deco and Mediterranean buildings that is now a National Historic District, will strengthen a broad mix of businesses, from the Old Post Office to hotels and apartment houses. In reinforcing the Art Deco theme, architect Robert Venturi has worked out guidelines to widen the sidewalks, cover blank walls with Art Deco murals, add palm trees, and capture the tropical flavor of the area and climate through the use of evocative pastel colors.

Orchard Street in New York is one long bargain basement. Clothes hang over the sidewalk like banners in the breeze. Casually dressed as well as elegant people walk along the narrow sidewalks between designer merchandise and a jumble of other goods. As for the peddlers, they add color and festivity. It is a celebration to the eye, and to clean it up in the name of aesthetic purity would be to undermine the reasons so many different people go there.

While the common denominator found in all streets is their people and activities, the degree of recognition of a street's theme varies considerably. Some streets appear to have no theme; other times it's there but hard to define. Sometimes, it's easy to recognize a theme because your street is so unique.

The Well-defined Theme

The well-defined street is the street that stands out; its uniqueness is readily visible. It is distinguished from other streets by its architecture, its street life, or the way it runs through town, from a splendid line to an intriguing series of curves or bends like Sunset Boulevard, by its relationship to adjacent buildings, streets, and major open areas like Fifth Avenue in New York.

Steiner Street in San Francisco has its own beat. Here is an emphatic repetition of the turn-of-the-century Victorian-housing style, with gabled roofs, bay windows, and decorative detailing accentuated by jolts of electric color. A proper house with a splash of purple! This is pure theater and brilliantly done.

In Nantucket, Massachusetts, color again is part of the theme but without the electric jolt—

Steiner Street, San Francisco

The curves and signs define the theme of Sunset Boulevard, Los Angeles

The theme of the Broadways,
San Francisco (above)
and New York City (below)
is big, bright electric signs.

Varying levels on Union St.
San Francisco, adds to its uniqueness.

this time the colors are subdued. The architectural code requires white paint for the clapboard exteriors, thus perpetuating the colonial image of the town. The white, with trim of gray, echoes the landscape and the sea beyond.

Beacon Hill, in Boston, and Society Hill, in Philadelphia, also reflect their strong heritage. Gas lamps, cobblestone paving, colored wooden shutters, wrought-iron railings, and brick houses spell out the themes.

Sunset Boulevard as it winds up into Hollywood and the Broadways (New York's and San Francisco's) are places that call out to you with Edison's successor to the carnival barker—big, bright, flashing electric signs. The theme is bold, honest, and straightforward, for these streets are in the excitement business.

The theme is just as apparent on some residential streets, such as Lombard Street in San Francisco and the streets in Venice, California. Exotic landscaping makes both these examples so strong that they linger in the memory for years. The homes in Venice share yards of stunning color separated by low wooden fences visible to the pedestrians along the street. Yard after yard of flowers and shrubs give the impression of a continuous public garden descending toward the waterfront. A few hundred miles to the north,

steep, winding Lombard Street is a succession of sharp turns that seem to have been cut into an enormous flower bed that ties the street together. Houses, cars, and flowers creep downhill. It is like driving through a picture postcard.

Not every street, not even most streets, make you feel as though you are driving, or walking, through a special place. You would never write home about them, saying, "Wish you were here." You must be familiar with streets, including yours back home, that have, to borrow from Gertrude Stein, "no there, there."

Such streets could be anywhere, anywhere. We know them as the commercial streets or strips—edged or, more aptly, encrusted with fast-food, chain-style outlets, discount stores, gas stations, parking lots, super- and not-so-supermarkets, and signs. Such streets usually have little or no architectural interest, and yet, as vehemently as some may rebel against such creeping chaos, they do have people and they do have activities—obviously supplying some sort of satisfaction to many Americans. If your own street happens to be of this kind, can you "save" it? Should you get involved? The fact that there are people and activities that appear to thrive on each other—"architectural interest" or not—suggests that a foundation for trying to improve it is there.

Lombard Street, San Francisco

Venice, California

Broadway, Los Angeles, is rich with Mexican flavor and active stores.

The Not-so-obvious Theme

The main focus in this book is neither just the street with great architecture nor the run-of-the-mill commercial strip. The concern here is with the retail street that is the core of its neighborhood — a street where the concentration of people and their activities contribute as much to the street as do its physical elements.

The theme of these streets, therefore, may not be immediately recognized or easily pinpointed. Yet you know it's there — you can feel it. While architecture, balconies, roofs, bay windows, and wide sidewalks may be what you see along the streets, it is the mix of people who socialize next to a popular drugstore or in boutiques that con-

tributes to the street's uniqueness. Such activities may often be taken for granted or overlooked; they are not as monolithic or measurable as architecture is. Don't take for granted the people and business vitality along your street; deserted streets are sad and unsafe. In your proposal, consider the crowds that are there already; after all, you want to motivate them to stay and come back.

In addition to active street life, many streets that are candidates for revitalization offer quite handsome architecture that has simply been buried under signs, soot, or haphazard layers of paint. Often by restoring such a street and upgrading signs, shop windows, and doorways, you will bring out the street's intrinsic character and make it a more handsome place.

On these kinds of streets, search for clues in the character, charm, and history that have been covered up. Recycling old buildings for new uses was the key for what happened on Main Street in Corning, New York, and not unlike what happened in Aurora, Illinois, where businesses were closing at the rate of two a month until, five years ago, the merchants found that *enhancing* the charm of older buildings helps to attract people downtown. Often, architectural detailing is hidden under large tin signs. Discovering these details is much like discovering intricate wood detailing on your fireplace after removing many coats of paint.

Then there are other trends that can pop up unpredictably to affect a street's theme. On Broadway, in Los Angeles, the influx of Mexicans played a role in the transformation of the area; now the stores' activities that had once been indoors extend right out onto the street, making it almost impossible to tell where the sidewalks end and the stores begin. When merchants place their wares outside, the street becomes a spontaneous, colorful mall. The street qualities resulting from this kind of ad hoc interaction are often more inviting and invigorating than a modern mall of the sleekest design.

In Little Italy, the narrow streets are used intensively. Friends meet in the cafes over espresso. From tenement windows, mothers watch children dodge between tourists. Each year, the streets become the stage for the San Gennaro and San Antonio festivals. Before the revitalization plan, these festivals were holidays that came and went. But observing the success of these limited street closings, and their impact on the neighborhood, inspired the planners to close the street every weekend during the summer, thus recreating the festival mood on a regular basis. The extension of sidewalk cafes, the addition of a bocci ball court on a vacant lot, and a flurry of new banners added to the vibrance of life that was already there.

Maybe your street has vacant lots that could be reclaimed to create open spaces for people to mingle freely under canvases stretched between buildings. Or maybe your street has a landscaped strip in the middle of the street bed, like the Broadway Mall on the Upper West Side of New York, where senior citizens socialize on sunny days; or like Commonwealth Avenue in the Back Bay district of Boston, where people, young and old, sit to watch cars and pedestrians and to simply absorb one of the most gracious urban vistas in America. This activity has become the neighborhood spectator sport. In both these streets, the malls could be developed as a major resource.

As you search for your street theme, take advantage of its special physical properties. There are scores of cities and towns around the country that were initially laid out with very wide streets to allow room for horses and carriages to turn around. Ample space may thus be available for new uses. Often the ingredients for success are in the place itself. What is needed is an open mind and a creative sense in order to grasp the opportunities that are there.

The most important consideration is to recognize your street theme and strengthen it by building upon its existing activities. In this process of discovering the remarkable qualities of your street you will soon find out that one singular element does not alone constitute a theme. Many streets have interesting individual elements that with imagination and ability can be linked together for the magic in them to appear.

Olvera Street, L.A., combines unique scale, open space and ethnic flavor.

East 116th St., N.Y.C., derives its character from merchandise display and its Spanish ambiance.

Hollywood Blvd., Los Angeles

Hollywood Boulevard, for example, is pure nostalgia. The gold star emblems embedded in the sidewalk must have added to the thrill of Hollywood in the Thirties. But these gold stars alone can't do it anymore. The use of the great movie houses along the street has vanished; new activities have to be found to recycle the buildings along the lines of the original theme. Hollywood Boulevard can regain its glory and economic vitality by integrating new uses with its old symbolic meaning. The theme of Hollywood Boulevard, while associated with the stars, needs a more comprehensive approach to recapture its real character of previous days.

While there are several ways to revitalize a street, don't make your street into something it isn't. Often there's a tendency for designers to be cute and attempt to remake a street in the image of some street in, say, Europe. A Swiss Village, which has great charm in the Alps where it belongs, seems bizarre in Colorado or northern

Michigan, where native terrain and history could well yield a more home-grown theme. A Mediterranean stucco village gets much of its character from the strong sun and unique light and so does a waterfront village in New England, but in its own different way. The Disneylands and Disney Worlds may be places of inspiration, simulating worlds of the past or future, but do not try to create cardboard copies of a theme or cultural image that seems forced upon your own street's character or that is simply corny.

A waterfront street, for instance, does not need to have its trash cans and street lamps shaped like tugboats in order to be successful. In effect you'd be making an imitation waterfront out of one that already exists. Remember — there's nothing like the real thing. After all, you want your street to be something that you can call your own.

If your street, like many around the country, has no unique physical features, but is more the typical commercial strip where vast parking lots separate one establishment from the other, the challenge of creating a sense of place may be harder. You may seek to create nodes of pedestrian activities rather than to force the development of a continuous, linear street. Look for places along the street where people naturally get together. The element always in your favor is human energy; look for inspiration from the people who use the street.

The Boardwalk in Atlantic City, New Jersey, with its rich 1930's-style architecture.

Headhouse Square, Philadelphia

Corning, New York

Royal Promenade, New Orleans

West 42nd St., New York City

The Proposal Reflects Your Theme

Now that you've defined your theme, you are ready to develop your proposal, where your creative ideas and the solutions to practical problems merge in the form of a plan.

In collecting data, you have become familiar with both the positive and the problematic aspects of your street. You have gotten to know its people and the particular attractions around which the crowds congregate. You've become acquainted with the dimly lit corners and the spots that are flooded by sunlight. You have pinpointed the dilapidated facades, the buildings in need of restoration, the vacant lots — and their possible uses. The plans that you and your task force are going to draw up must express this overall knowledge, projecting and illustrating what you have analyzed to be your street's special needs.

Develop your plan in two stages: first, a general overview, then a more specific, detailed plan. The basic plan ties all of the street's components together so that you get a comprehensive visual impression of the end product. This general plan — really a design concept — includes both permanent and temporary solutions. Temporary solutions and incremental steps should be used as catalysts for the long-term plan. A one-time, organized painting project for all storefronts, with the merchants pitching in, can become the basis for an ongoing preservation campaign.

Target your plan to develop the "sense of place" — the theme. You can do it by strengthening the most remarkable features and integrating them into all that you have learned about your street. Develop visual links — connections that unify your street and reinforce its substance, its motif. It is not enough to make one shop attractive; you want one action to have an eventual impact on adjoining properties.

There are several kinds of links that bind a street or a neighborhood together — those that connect groups of activities and those that connect special or significant places. In Old San Diego and El Pueblo Viejo (Santa Barbara's Mexican-American historic district), the visual associations are accomplished through the coordinated use of building materials: red roof tiles, the repetition of arches, desert landscaping, vintage signage, and rustic street furniture. In Palm Springs, rows of palm trees planted along its main street, Palm Canyon, unify the street's image.

If your street has awnings scattered along 60 per cent of its front, vote to continue these awnings along the entire street facade. Further, the repetition of the same color for the awnings will help distinguish your street from others. A network of pedestrian pathways, spotted with street lights and unique graphics, can act as a link between a downtown commercial center and the waterfront. In Boston, the newly revived Quincy Market, City Hall, and harbor frontage are linked together through a network of plazas where people stroll, sit, dine, and listen to music. Visual links can be symbols of a network of activities that are the framework of your theme.

Architecture creates visual links.
Walnut Street, Philadelphia

Developing visual connections, though, does not always express the street's theme. While the repetition of harmonious elements may be one way to unify your street, on the contrary, your street may be distinguished from the rest by its ad hoc, jumbled quality. This was considered a distinct plus along the stretch of Chicago's South Dearborn Street known as Printing House Row, where the variety of structures included a number of landmark buildings of different styles housing a mix of shops and services. While the long-neglected buildings are restored for residential and commerical uses, the older printing establishments are being encouraged to stay through special tax incentives. Thus the old sense of the street, derived from its multi-functional uses, will be main-

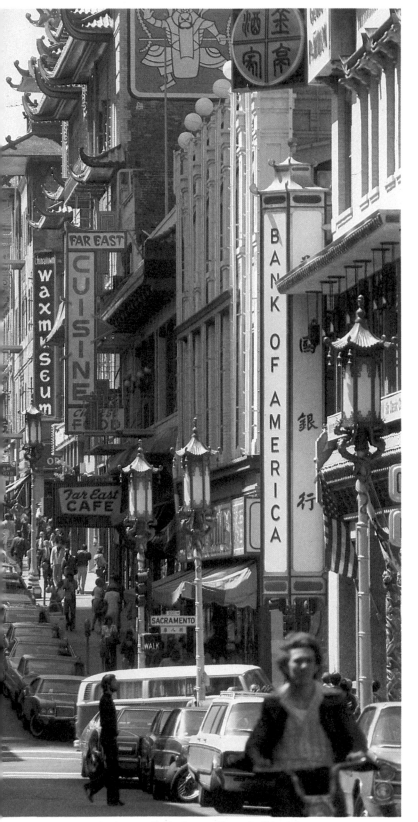

A strong ethnic theme threads through Chinatown, San Francisco

tained and will help attract newcomers. As on Printing House Row, the difference and not the sameness of your street can become the focus of your inspiration. Rather than just unifying your street, you may want to accent its diversity.

By now, you have decided either to reinforce the unity of your street's theme or to accentuate the street's diversity, or you may have come up with a new creative vision that was not obvious from the start, but that reinforces the street's existing values. Regardless, the understanding of people's needs and the analysis of the street's physical properties are the keys to developing your proposal within the realistic framework of the street's potential.

At this point of the process you may opt to create a one-day special event along your street, the first step in making more people aware of the potential of their own street. You will also be presenting the design concept through simple visual aides showing photo montages of before-and-after views of the street, to show people how the "three-dimensional room" — their street — would look under various alternatives expressing their street's uniqueness. As people recognize their landmark buildings, identify their favorite restaurants, and begin to appreciate their improved open space, the presentation will take on a personal meaning for them.

Be frank about available funding resources, from both public and private sectors, so that community and government representatives will get an early idea of the costs involved, and who will pay for what in the various alternatives.

Do not be too possessive about your first proposal. Leave room for compromise and a fresh, even unexpected, input. In the process you will discover that your final proposal may not be the exact one you started with. The added input of the participants will help mold your concept as it matures.

You are now far ahead in your quest. You have collected your data, discovered your theme, investigated funding potentials, and developed a proposal that sparked the imagination of the entire neighborhood. The time has come to translate your aspirations into reality. Implementation — making it happen — is the last piece of the puzzle.

SHORT-TERM IMPLEMENTATION

The Nitty-Gritty

Implementation is translating the design concept into reality. A plan is a fantasy if not implemented. There are four parts to this process —budget, management, maintenance, and construction.

Implementation will often include both short-term and long-term improvements. Short-term improvements provide immediate visible impact and almost always involve less expense. Simple steps—planting flowers, painting fire hydrants, installing bike racks, painting murals on blank walls, or closing the street for a day—can have a major psychological effect on the community. They can see that something is happening and then will realize how much more can happen.

No plan, regardless of how elaborate, should have a time frame stretched out to the point where a major population turnover will occur before completion. For one thing, it is important that the people who have participated in the process see the fruits of their labor. For another, new people coming in will simply have less enthusiasm for a project that somebody else started.

The long-term action plan is usually more ambitious, more costly, and more complicated. It requires the use of legal and financial tools and is a way to insure that the character you have created by your immediate actions will be carried on and strengthened in the future. Zoning, facade easements, and tax abatements are some of the long-term implementation techniques that will help you in reaching such goals.

A street's short-term improvement should be considered the first step toward the long-term project. In fact, the short-term steps should be viewed chiefly as the generator to help get the long-term work started. An immediate action may focus attention on the quality of buildings, but it will not assure either their preservation or their relationship to new buildings on the street. That's why the total plan should cover both short- and long-term improvements; the one helps lead to the other.

Aside from being highly visible, improvements should also be economically feasible. Projects that depend on a single extravagant budget often never get off the planner's shelf. They turn the community off. This happened in Newkirk when an architect came up with a $3 million project to deck the entire plaza. Newkirk didn't have the $3 million and he didn't have a more modest alternate plan. Immediate result: nothing.

In Little Italy, the street closing was used to get support for more permanent legislation to preserve the neighborhood's character. It had an instant effect. The weekend mall was the catalyst that brought public attention to the community's attempts at self-help. The street became the unifying element between the city and the community-based organizations.

The initiative for a project can come from a variety of groups; the government, the community, or the Chamber of Commerce. It doesn't matter who originates the idea. The key is that implementation should be made a joint venture between public and private interests. Since the street bed and sidewalks are often public property and the buildings are privately owned, the interests of the two groups are intertwined. Past experience has proven that the community's attitude toward property that is solely managed and improved by the city is not the same as when the community itself participates in both management and implementation. In fact, economic involvement, no matter how small, will give the community a sense that the street belongs to them.

The division of responsibility—who maintains what, and who pays for what—has to be spelled out from the start. When tasks overlap between the partners, many projects are begun but not completed. In light of the numbers of participants and complexity in the implementation process, outlining specifically the exact responsibilities of each group is crucial. It makes the work viable.

New street plans often add modern street furnishings that need more maintenance than the city's day-to-day service can cover. Make sure it is clear what your city agrees to maintain and what the community will do. You may decide on the "adopt a tree" program, by which every merchant is responsible for the tree planted in front of his shop, or a revolving fund may be set up by your merchants' group to pay for an extra cleaning shift.

Preparation of the Budget

Preparation of the budget is the first task in your immediate implementation plan. Cost is usually the chief factor in determining project priorities. The budget is the first document that you will be asked to present to any major corporation or financial backer. To them, the numbers may be the most tangible aspect of your project. Prepare a flexible budget which includes costs for a variety of design alternatives and allows for a realistic timetable for project development.

Your task force should provide minimum and maximum budget alternatives that give the community at large a variety of choices. While the maximum budget allocation may be the most desirable one, alternatives have to be ready should you need to adjust the plan to a more pragmatic solution. Do not, however, lose the integrity of your plan in the process. A flexible budget should not lead you to a piecemeal approach. Although your plan may consist of elements from several alternatives, make sure that the final plan is a comprehensive one.

In Newkirk Plaza, for example, the original brick paving to cover the entire plaza would have used up two thirds of the total budget. The community, equipped with budget alternatives, was able to study a number of options and weigh them according to their means. They finally decided to pave only part of the plaza and spend the rest of the funds on other items. Since the original plan anticipated this alternative and included a manageable timetable, the change in the paving plan did not consequently affect the major concept for the plaza.

Alternatives should reflect the cost of materials, manufacturing, and installation, as well as contracting fees and management costs. No budget is too detailed. Prices of different materials for the same item should be weighed against their durability and maintenance requirements.

Using street furniture that the city already carries in stock is one way to save money. Sometimes a minor change in standard equipment will give you a ''new look'' without the added cost of custom-made items. A small iron crossbar on a standard lighting fixture, for example, may become the support structure for hanging planters with flowers. (Also, it is easier to replace and maintain standard city items.)

All budgets should include maintenance and contingency costs. You will probably find both government and private institutions more likely to fund capital improvements that include within their budget maintenance funds, than just pay for maintenance alone. People would rather pay for building something than for just cleaning it. Therefore, when you seek funding for capital improvements make sure that you include both maintenance and basic construction costs. It is also a good idea for special funds to be earmarked for maintenance purposes, as in special tax assessment districts, where such funds are directed to a specific area — such as your street. Inflation may also have a major impact on your plan. A 10 to 20 per cent contingency allowance should be included to absorb the rising costs of labor and equipment. Likely increases in prices and construction costs are another reason to implement your plan as swiftly as possible.

Phasing: Phasing of a project is breaking it up into manageable steps within a feasible timetable. It provides for flexibility that makes it easier to get additional funding later. It also offers an immediate first step that demonstrates to the community that things are happening right away.

The ability to execute a plan in phases is essential. First, it is easier to get some degree of funding to cover a small project than the whole lump sum for a long-term plan. Second, phasing gives the community the opportunity to juggle improvement costs and decide on new priorities in light of changing needs. Third, phasing makes it possible to go to funding sources with an accomplishment at hand to establish credibility. Fourth, phasing allows for implementing manageable projects in size and cost. But most important is the community sense that it can get something done. Nothing will undermine community morale more than a project that gets half finished and dies.

Finally, phasing may also provide environmental and economic benefits. If all the work was done at a single time, the day-to-day activity of the street might be jeopardized. Imagine paving the street, steam cleaning the buildings, painting the walls, putting in new street lighting, and installing canopies all at once. The uncoordinated scheduling could bring the operating businesses to revolt, and the street revitalization to a halt.

Whether or not phasing is possible or practical depends on the project. Sometimes in large historic districts where building cleaning and restoration are involved, it is generally less expensive if the work is contracted to be done all at once. Or if a street's repavement in brick is part of the street plan, phasing such a project may entail longer periods of construction work, disrupting and inconveniencing the pedestrians and merchants. It may be difficult to phase a plan that includes a major transportation system. The construction of New York's Second Avenue subway project, which was done in phases but never completed, left a lot of unfilled holes in the ground when the budget was cut in the midst of its construction. Therefore, while in most cases phasing a project will benefit your street plan, be aware of the unique conditions when its application is limiting.

In addition to phasing, a flexible budget also allows the community to shop for the best plan within the limits of what it can afford. Sometimes professional planners assume on their own how much a community can afford or underestimate what a community can undertake. This may be unwise, since only the community knows the realm of what it can accomplish, and often, assuming there is little money available can be an error. A creative, detailed plan may attract additional funding that you had not anticipated from the start. You will also find that there is nothing like a detailed budget to help you in the search for funds.

Funding Sources

Discovering funds is a challenge, and the cardinal rule is to leave no stone unturned. Often funding that is actually available for street revitalization is hidden in funds that are allocated directly to other purposes. Within Urban Mass Transit Administration grants, which are allocated for highway improvements, and within Housing and Urban Development funds, which are earmarked primarily for housing, money is available

The Transit Mall, Portland, Oregon

for other uses. Search through these grant descriptions and others and you will find that some funding can be allocated for street improvements and pedestrian amenities.

In Portland, Oregon, the well-designed transit mall, which includes innovative street furniture, decorative paving, and other amenities for pedestrians, was funded by Department of Transportation monies that were originally earmarked for highway improvement. In this case, "highway improvement" was creatively interpreted to include an extended street improvement program, which in turn transformed the image of the entire downtown area.

Moral: The funding for your street improvements may be hidden in highway grants. Make sure to look for opportunities and grants that at first sight don't seem to apply directly to you.

Logically, you would expect to find at least

one person in the city government in charge of grants allocated specifically for street improvement, but that is rarely the case. You might seek help from the public official who represents your street (councilman, assemblyman, or congressman). Large cities, such as New York, have a full-time representative in Washington, D.C., who is in charge of securing grants. In your case, you may need to assign a person to research available grants that apply to your street. Whatever you do, you will have to be resourceful and maybe a little ingenious.

As important as government funding is to you, increased competition for shrinking government dollars (often available only in the form of matching funds) makes private funding crucial to your street-improvement program. As indicated earlier in this chapter, sources of funding may include businesses that have a financial interest in your street: major banks, department stores, or a utility company. Also look for help from large corporations or foundations located outside your neighborhood, especially those that have shown an interest in community affairs. For example, the Ford Foundation has recently launched a national program in support of community revitalization.

And last but not least, go to the merchants or the residents on the street itself. Their contributions may be small, but it is essential to get them economically involved in the project. Remember, the experience around the country has demonstrated that when the people who live and work on the street don't contribute anything to the revitalization effort, they do not feel as involved with the changes.

Management

The importance of a comprehensive approach and the need for a well-managed financial plan in your implementation process has already been stressed; such a management plan is imperative. An experienced group to carry it out is essential: without a vehicle to implement your management plan, and professional "know-how," managing your project may become a nightmare.

Management includes a wide range of activities: establishing rapport with government agencies, securing funding, selecting contractors,

monitoring government funding requirements, and such daily operations as supervising construction, ordering and coordinating the delivery of street furniture, scheduling street activities, paying contractors, soliciting publicity through the media, and representing community interests.

Local development corporations, community task forces, and government agencies can share responsibility for management tasks. But organizational experience varies from locality to locality and according to the scale of the project. In Philadelphia, a special non-profit management corporation was established for the management and maintenance of "The Gallery," a mixed-use, multilevel shopping and transportation center, thus allowing the various groups with an interest in the project — the merchants, the Redevelopment Authority, and the city — to cope with this complex undertaking. Where no management group exists, one must be created. Right from the start, it has to be clear to all involved who is in charge.

It is easier for the community to participate in the decision-making process than it is to find qualified volunteers who can manage the program on a day-to-day basis. Management is a full-time job. Therefore, a successful project requires a full-time manager. This is one time when professional help is essential, and spending money to hire someone has its definite rewards.

During the first year of the Mulberry Street project, management responsibilities were jointly carried out by LIRA (Little Italy Restoration Association) and the Urban Design Group of the City of New York, under a dynamic manager who was greatly responsible for following through on every detail. However, LIRA membership came from neighborhood business leaders and residents with little management experience and limited time; and when the full-time manager left, it became clear that such important tasks as searching for funds, dealing with manufacturers, negotiating with city agencies, and expediting the day-to-day progress lacked the full attention needed. At this point, a professional manager would have been a prudent community investment.

At Newkirk Plaza, a management team was formed from members of two community organizations and the Transit Authority. This proved an efficient and well-thought-out arrangement, and the project seems to be moving ahead more or less on schedule.

In Far Rockaway, on the other hand, the management team, which included thirty representatives of various city agencies and community groups, was effective in making decisions but was too large to manage the project. The lack of a professional manager in Far Rockaway has kept implementation from moving ahead at any great pace.

Maintenance

There is nothing glamorous about maintenance. Realistically, maintenance responsibilities should be divided between the public and private sectors. Regardless of who is responsible, a comprehensive plan is necessary to cover daily as well as long-term maintenance.

If your plan includes special items outside the city's usual maintenance tasks, the city simply may not agree to take on the additional costs. Don't depend on public agencies for the maintenance of newly added street items. In Little Italy, providing extra lighting for the banners became a problem. The first year the banners were lit; during the second year, service was terminated because the city would not assume the cost for the additional energy. Cleaning banners, watering new trees and flowers, and maintaining ornamental lighting may therefore have to be done by a private group.

In Far Rockaway, Brooklyn Gas and Electric Company agreed to pay the energy costs for decorative pedestrian lights. But since their standard street lamps were not used, the community had to pay for maintenance and new bulbs.

Sometimes, joint public and private maintenance works well. In Newkirk, private owners maintained the storefronts. The Transit Authority maintained the plaza deck, since it was located on Transit land, and the city maintained the adjacent streets.

It is hard to find volunteers in the community for maintenance work. And once they do volunteer, you may run into problems. In Little Italy it was a major problem to find volunteers to move the planters and reopen the street to traffic at the end of the weekend street-closing. Watering the trees also presented difficulties. At first there was a group called the "Green Thumbs" who volunteered to keep the trees alive. That program soon fizzled out. An "adopt a tree" program was instituted instead, where each storeowner became a "foster parent" to a nearby tree. The owners developed a more personal response in keeping the greenery alive.

The "adoption" technique, in fact, could even be extended to an adopt-a-building program. An institution such as a church or bank might undertake the maintenance responsibilities for a noteworthy building on your street. This would insure their ongoing participation in community projects. You may even be fortunate and find an individual willing to maintain another part of your street, such as a small park or a fountain. Be creative in addressing your maintenance problems. Discover new approaches! But the maintenance approach you select should depend on the amount you can afford, and on the street's special circumstances.

As you plan your maintenance program, consider both one-time and daily maintenance responsibilities. One-time maintenance involves such items as cleaning building facades perhaps once every twenty years, or replanting trees after a windstorm. Daily maintenance involves the chores of street upkeep. Seasonal planting, sanitation, replacement of missing bricks after a utility installation are just a few examples. Make sure you know the full extent in terms of tasks and costs involved. Do not assume these things are understood without saying.

To minimize costs (or at least to keep them under control), familiarize yourself with the durability and upkeep of various materials and the methods of cleaning buildings and streets.

Durability and upkeep of materials: While a good piece of artwork may be a large initial expense, it takes more effort to keep up a tree than a piece of sculpture. And natural-wood furniture, though costly, does not have to be painted every year. It is wrong to think that you have to choose between attractiveness and durability. There are many attractive, durable materials on the market.

One learns a great deal about maintenance from

experience. In Little Italy, banners, instead of flowers, were placed on fire escapes in order to eliminate the work involved in watering. As it turned out, the banners required efforts that were just not anticipated. Fireproof nylon banners were selected over felt, but what was not foreseen was that nylon banners would need cleaning every year. The community, trying to be thrifty, washed the banners after the first summer. The colors faded and the banners became useless. Another unforeseen maintenance problem involved hanging the banners. It was discovered too late that rigging is incredibly expensive, since riggers in New York, like many other workers, are unionized.

The debate over the selection of planters, which were used to close the streets to traffic, revolved around upkeep. While concrete planters discouraged vandalism and theft, they were too heavy to move at the end of the weekend when the street was reopened to traffic. On the other hand, expensive redwood planters were durable and lightweight. The natural-wood finish aged to a deep, rich, brown color which added to the aesthetic image of the streetscape. Equipped with industrial wheels, the planters were easily moved. Ironically, however, the advantage of mobility caused a problem. Out of thirty-six planters, two disappeared in the first two weeks.

You may not want to think about this, but vandalism and theft are major considerations in your street-improvement plan. In Little Italy, the commuity favored free-standing chairs for sidewalk cafes. But free-standing furniture has been known to disappear. Unless you have an endless supply of free furniture, all movable furniture will need to be stored when not in use.

If your plan includes umbrellas, the type of base and the fabric you select make a difference. Though most umbrellas are anchored to the sidewalk through the center of a table, it is still necessary to use additional weight in cases of high wind or uneven ground surfaces. Special canisters can be designed to be filled with water in order to balance the weight. When the time comes to select your fabric, you may be tempted to use plastic. While plastic is indeed more durable, it is unquestionably less attractive than canvas. The attractiveness of canvas may justify the added cost (not unlike deciding between using plastic flowers and fresh-cut ones). Regardless of the material, this is the time to have some fun and to use your imagination. A change in color could express a change in season.

The more trees and flowers you have on your street, the more care they will require. Nothing is more demoralizing than a tree that is dying. While it is undeniably more expensive to buy a large tree, you will find that in the long run it is easier to care for a tree of, say, 3½–4 inches caliper than a smaller one.

The maintenance of trees and plants changes with geographical area; climatic conditions and water availability differ throughout the country. In the east, green ivy is fairly easy to keep, but seasonal flowers require much work. Ivy seems to withstand urban pollution. (Ivy will outlive us all.) Remember that while flowering trees add color to the environment, they bloom only twice a year in most areas. Make sure when you select your trees that you choose some that allow for the visibility of your shops from both sides of the street.

The New York City Planning Commission recently published a booklet called "Trees," which outlines maintenance conditions for over one hundred trees in the urban environment. Other cities and states most likely have similar information applying to their area. (The Department of Agriculture or your local garden club may assist you.)

Cleaning Buildings and Streets: The least expensive means of cleaning surfaces along a streetfront is to paint them. Weatherproof exterior paint is best for jobs like storefronts, graphics, signage, and blank walls. Painting is simple but requires periodic repainting. It can be done by high school kids or professionals. But don't become so enthusiastic that you cover up architectural detail and rich textures.

Buildings of architectural quality will require more sophisticated methods of cleaning. Usually, private contractors specializing in such work will have to be hired. Your city probably has cleaning companies that provide services for many types of masonry surfaces and graffiti removal.

The two most widely used cleaning methods

for masonry are water pressure and steam cleaning. Water pressure, a chemical process, is most effective when used for heavy cleaning of those facades that have been blemished by several coats of paint. Steam cleaning is used to clean brick and stone but is not effective in removing paint.

Sandblasting will bruise brick and soften stone surfaces. Therefore, its use should be limited to very hard materials, such as cast-iron and granite under heavy coats of paint and dirt.

In addition to cleaning, masonry buildings may also need to be spot-painted, (i.e., cleared of residue that gathers in mortar joints) and weatherproofed with paint.

These cleaning methods, recently used in London, Paris, and New York to "rediscover" the great buildings of the past, are now also catching on in small and large cities everywhere. On your own street, cleaning and lighting your noteworthy buildings and getting individual owners to repaint adjacent properties, will be a dramatic first step in changing your neighborhood.

A major concern, of course, is the cleaning of the sidewalks and the street itself. Although this is a city responsibility, your new plan may require additional help, including manpower or equipment, from private groups. Try to integrate your extra maintenance requirements into your design concept at an early stage.

Changing the traffic patterns can increase trash pile-ups, and street closings have been known to double normal trash loads. With weekend street closings, you should also expect to pay sanitation workers overtime for Sundays. Newkirk merchants purchased a mechanical sweeper and hired a porter.

You may designate central locations for garbage collection so that vacant lots and sidewalks don't become buried under refuse. Or else you may want to limit your sanitation collections to certain times of the day.

It is best to use standard trash containers from the city, since these will facilitate replacement and collection. Find innovative ways to integrate the containers into your street concept. You may elect to design a container to match your planters, one that will hold the standard trash receptacle from the city, for example. Use colors and materials that complement your other street furniture. When selecting street furniture, it is best to use products that are on the open market, since these are easy to replace. This rule also applies to street paving units.

The kind of maintenance program you adopt will vary with your specific plan. But after your street has been improved, poor maintenance will become even more obvious. Don't let your efforts be jeopardized at the eleventh hour by a simple lack of attention and care. Fortunately, once your street has become an attractive place to be, its people will cherish it and treat it with respect as though it was an extension of their own homes.

2

MULBERRY STREET IN LITTLE ITALY

Mulberry Street in Little Italy may appear, at first glance, to be just another New York neighborhood retail street. Yet, every September for the last fifty years, millions of people have flocked to Mulberry Street to celebrate the San Gennaro festival. Overnight, a transformation occurs. In honor of San Gennaro, the third-century bishop of Benevento, Italy, a ten day long celebration changes the small, gray, cluttered street into an explosion of lights, color, and music. It is this annual occasion that finally created the momentum and the inspiration for a revitalization of the whole area. The drab look of everyday Little Italy, with its low tenements and unpainted facades, crowded with trucks, local businesses and small factories, did not project its underlying strengths. The physical condition of the area did not express the richness of its cultural qualities, social customs, and ethnic flavor. It was the festival that highlighted the great cultural assets and emphasized its attractive scale.

Of the many Italian enclaves in America, New York's Little Italy is the oldest. Since the early nineteenth century, it has been home for hundreds of thousands who came to this country. Although many waves of immigrants had settled in the neighborhood between Broadway and the Bowery, it was the Italians who stayed and whose

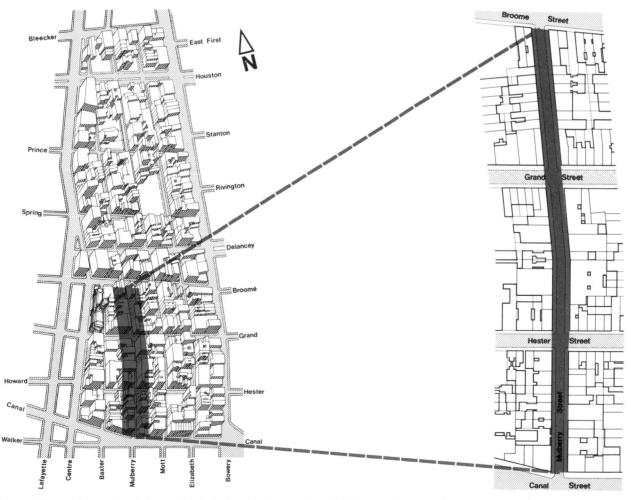

Above: Three dimensional view of Little Italy with the section of Mulberry Street under study.
Left: Night view of San Gennaro Festival on Mulberry Street.

heritage transformed the area into a slice of the old country. Social customs and religious traditions were transported into the New World setting.

Coming from Naples and Sicily, where the climate was warm, the new settlers were accustomed to being outdoors. Thus the narrow streets of Little Italy became cluttered with outdoor activities. Pushcarts, sidewalk cafes, and organ grinders congested the sidewalks. The *Harper's Weekly* of 1895 described the area as "the most picturesque, squalid, delapidated, thoroughly interesting and lively foreign colony in New York City."

Little Italy was the starting point for many Italians who joined their countrymen already living in that neighborhood and working hard to better their lives. Many moved on to Long Island and other suburbs. But today several thousands of Italians still reside in Little Italy, and more than ever the area maintains a symbolic link to Italian heritage.

Little Italy and its neighbors

It is not only Italians who identify with Little Italy today. The Chinese from the adjacent neighborhood in south Chinatown work, live, and go to school there.

Chinatown's history is comparatively recent. In 1858, a Cantonese man named Ah Ken was the first to settle there. He opened a cigar shop on Park Row and made his home on Mott Street. As late as 1872 there were only twelve Chinese in the area, but by 1880, the number had increased to 700. Today the population of Chinatown is 135,000. It is therefore not surprising that in the last decade the Chinese have moved north into Little Italy as their population expanded.

In spite of this population shift, Little Italy, with Mulberry Street as its neighborhood core, has remained the most outstanding Italian center in this country. Although only 20,000 Italians presently remain in the area, the atmosphere of Little Italy retains its old-world traditions and ambience. Traces of the old country are still evident, especially in the patron-saint fiestas, the Social Clubs, and the strong family ties. The streets of Little Italy continue to be the main element of the neighborhood's social structure. You can learn about Italian geography from the streets of Little Italy. The Neapolitans moved to Mulberry Street, the Sicilians settled in Elizabeth Street, and on Mott Street families from Calabria resided. The many traditions of various Italian districts are still alive in Little Italy.

The residents make intensive use of the street as a focal interest point; enjoying their daily *passeggiata* or evening stroll, sitting on front stoops, looking out from windows above, and drinking espresso in small cafes. Specialty stores and business establishments with vintage nineteenth-century storefronts have been managed by the same families for generations. Mulberry Street remains the best source of Italian produce in New York City. Its restaurants, cafes, and Italian specialty shops carry national and regional food: cheeses, sausages, pasta, dried and fresh fish, special meat cuts, imported oils and spices, pastries, espresso, of course, and Italian books, records, and gifts. You can still wander into a restaurant and see a painted mural of the Sorrento

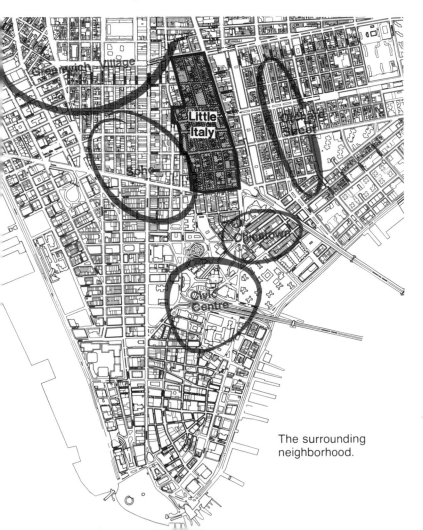

The surrounding neighborhood.

countryside or photos of Italian politicians from another century.

Each of the nearby neighborhoods also maintains unique customs; people come from all over the region to enjoy this variety. Within a ten-minute walk of Little Italy, you can latch onto the bargains and bravura of Orchard Street or get lost roaming through the galleries, antique shops, bookstores, and eateries of Soho, savor the many cuisines of Chinatown, or take in the mix of history and hedonism that is Greenwich Village. For the various ethnic groups who live there, the diversity of people who identify with it as dwellers, or the many visitors who delight in the neighborhood, Little Italy is considered the Italian core of this metropolitan area.

That is why, year after year, millions come for such events as the San Gennaro festival. Every September for ten days Mulberry Street is closed to cars and transformed into a midway celebration, the *Festa* of San Gennaro, the patron saint of Naples. The streets are decorated with wide strings of electric lights, creating a glittering frame of arches, and become one vast alfresco restaurant with stalls selling grilled sausages, clams on the half shell, pizza, zeppole, and ices. Games of chance offer prizes varying from stuffed dolls to bottles of Italian wine. While the children play on a street carousel, the elderly enjoy the traditional game of bocci nearby. Among the balloons and inexpensive souvenirs, original ceremonies from faraway villages in Italy are also taking places. In no time the shrine to San Gennaro is adorned with dollar bills from the many believers celebrating this joyful event.

This festival and the spirit of the Italian community behind it demonstrated that the yearly San Gennaro surge could be an ongoing benefit. It was an anchor for the idea that improving the condition and appearance of the building's sidewalks and storefronts was indeed basic to the overall revitalization of the area.

Geographic borders

The area occupied by Little Italy is little more than a mile north of the site of New Amsterdam, the first Dutch settlement of merchants and traders in New York, on the tip of Lower Manhattan.

A view of Mulberry Street in 1890

The first land was rural. In 1642 the Bowery (literally meaning a Colonial Dutch plantation) farms were laid out. By 1700 the general area bounded by Canal, where a canal ran in the old days, Houston Street, Broadway, and the Bowery was unified in one ownership, a farm owned by a nephew of Peter Stuyvesant. By 1800, the streets of what is now Little Italy had been plotted.

Traditionally the borders of Little Italy are Canal Street on the south, the Bowery on the east, Bleeker Street on the north, and Lafayette Street on the west. These familiar borders are not hard and fast barriers, but are recognized by informal consent and custom. For example, the San Gennaro Festival rarely extends to the portion of Mulberry Street south of Canal, which is ethnically recognized as Chinatown. While it is clear that neighborhoods overlap at borders, when you want to study a neighborhood, the establishment of imaginary lines allows you to concentrate on the specific designated area. The uniqueness of Little Italy is recognizable not by the five- and six-story railroad tenements that are predominant throughout the Lower East Side, but more by the active storefronts and by the way the Italians use their narrow streets, as if they are enjoying a village street in sunny Italy.

Certainly these streets as outdoor ''rooms'' are elemental to the whole neighborhood's character. Women, wearing black, bring chairs to the sidewalk to meet their friends; others stand at the window watching their children play for hours on end. News is passed along at entrances to men's social clubs; decisions are made on front stoops; different Italian dialects are detected on each corner. It is this social interaction, mixed with the aromas of Italy's best cooking from Naples to Milan, that attracts so many outsiders to roam about the area and sample some homemade pasta.

Six-story, late nineteenth century residential structures line the streets of Little Italy. While technically classified as "tenements" when they were built, many have great charm and interesting architectural detail. At street level one cannot miss the unique scale of the few remaining vintage cast-iron storefronts. Scattered between restaurants and the myriad specialty food stores are printing shops or garment factories. The balance of industry and residential above the ground level that is the neighborhood's core, combined with ground-level colorful storefronts and decorative restaurants for tourists, give Little Italy a diversity, an authenticity, and a dimension of mystery and unexpected finds.

Early community involvement

But charm and spirit alone cannot save a neighborhood. In the early 1970s the people of Little Italy came to the realization that they were facing serious problems. It is hard to discern how this realization occurred. There were many factors involved. The importance of ethnic neighborhoods had become a priority even for city government establishment. There was the reality of the physical dilapidation of housing and the lack of amenities in the area, the increasing traffic and pollution from industry, and, of course, the recognized but unexpressed fear of loss of Italian identity and pride as the Chinese population swelled and began expanding into the neighborhood.

It isn't clear why a certain moment is the right time to wake up a dormant community. In Little Italy it was a combination of factors. It may have been the threat of the Lower Manhattan Expressway plan, which would have replaced Little Italy

with a highway and large-scale developments, and the infiltration of the Chinese community; both served indirectly to unite the Italian community. But, as in all revitalization projects, the individual personalities involved made the difference. On the government end, the City Planning Commission Chairman was John Zuccotti, himself an Italian-American born in nearby Greenwich Village, who had a special interest in the neighborhood revitalization and a personal commitment to the area. There were the local residents and merchants who formed the Little Italy Restoration Association (known as LIRA), a nonprofit local development corporation with the purpose, according to member John Fretta, the pork store owner, "of restoring the soul and atmosphere of Little Italy, fanning a spark in the coal to keep it alive." Other members of LIRA were Mr. Vitale and Mr. Graddi, undertakers who, after a family feud, hadn't spoken to each other for forty years; Mr. Ianello, who owns Umberto's Clam House; Anna Capparelli, a housewife who was delivered by midwife to a fifth-generation family in Little Italy; Frank Russo, the Democratic district leader; and, of course, Father Maranacchi, representing the parishes in the area.

But LIRA was not the first local group to express concern about Little Italy's situation. As early as 1967, a group known as the Neighborhood Council to Combat Poverty (NCCP) was organizing to help people, beginning with getting essential services for senior citizens. By the time LIRA got involved, the NCCP was being acclaimed as one of the most effective social service community organizations in New York.

Thus economic interests and social needs were both represented in the first steps of Little Italy's revitalization process.

A historic meeting

At a town meeting at the local Bowery Savings Bank, the concept for revitalization was revealed for the first time and was received with applause. Contributions from one dollar to $1,000 were raised for LIRA. More vitally, the citizens of the area, in their first face-to-face encounter with John Zuccotti, Chairman of the City Planning Department, and Percy Sutton, the Borough

Mulberry Street before the street improvement: View looking north

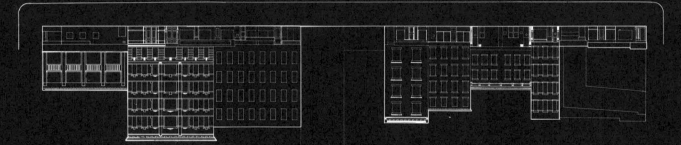

Canal st.

Hester st.

Above: Plan of existing conditions of Mulberry Street showing street bed, sidewalk and building elevations on both sides of street.

From left to right:

Sidewalk cafe at a noted pastry shop.

Parade during an Italian festival.

Time of friendly encounters.

Leisure time is spent sitting along the sidewalk, observing street activities.

The following page, left to right:

Tables and chairs to rest exhausted tourists.

Sea food add flavor and smell.

Homeland specialties color window shops.

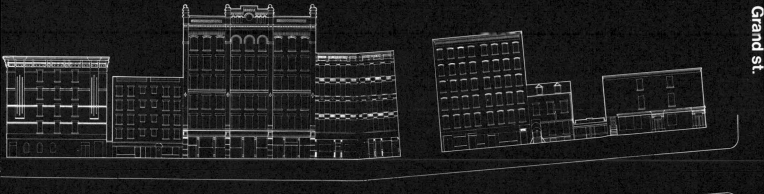

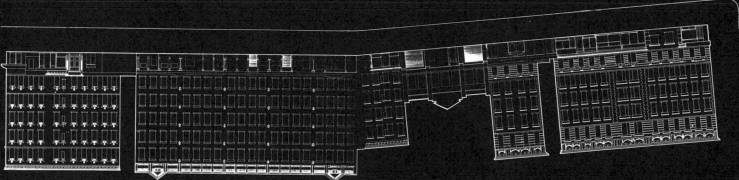

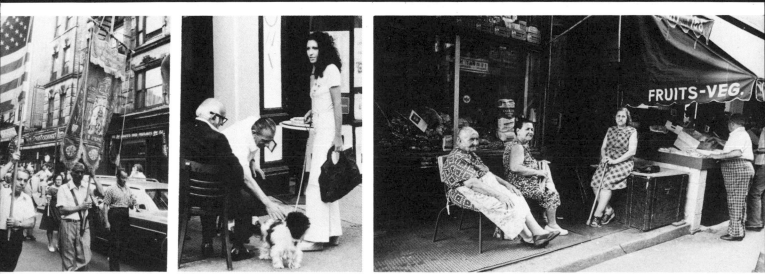

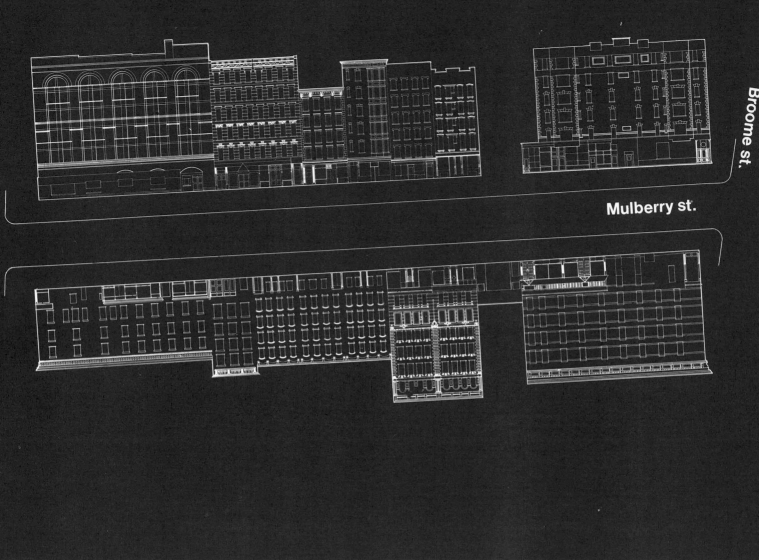

Broome st.

Mulberry st.

President of Manhattan, realized that government officials were interested in the area and understood what was at stake.

Anna Capparelli, who eventually became a major activist in LIRA, recalls the historical meeting of March 28, 1974. She says "I was in awe to see important men like John Zuccotti and Borough President Percy Sutton speaking to us about our area. It was mind boggling seeing all of these families and friends all excited, everyone making a little speech, talking about improving our area and about preparing corporate papers, presenting those little cards printed up in black and white with LIRA on them, like Lira, the money in Italy. They were talking about opening a community storefront. I will volunteer my services, I thought. We were going to have a new neighborhood. I could not believe it. The next thing I knew I was answering phones in the new storefront of the community at Grand Street."

Describing these first community meetings, Anna adds, "I was just so confused. Everything was new to me, especially those words *proposal, goals, alternatives,* I was at a blank. In the interim what we did was put together committees: committee for housing, committee for pedestrianization, committee for health, committee for education. The pedestrianization committee for the street mall was the most ambitious because it was something that was very visible. We may have talked about education, but the money was not there to build a school. The streets were there. They are for the people so this was the most vital realizable committee, and working on it gave us the feeling of the old country. So we worked very hard at it."

The Risorgimento Plan

Later that Spring, this group of enthusiastic citizens and LIRA, aided by government planners, launched a study of the area to develop specific recommendations for counteracting the evident economic and physical decline. This study was all the more pertinent because the City Planning Commission was already in the process of developing plans to designate SoHo, the adjacent artists' and manufacturing area, and Chinatown as unique neighborhood districts. The Urban Design

Group joined forces with LIRA to help formulate the original plan and set up a framework for communication and cooperation between the city's agencies and the community's leadership. The signals for resurgence that emerged through the renewed pride of the local community had triggered a partnership between government and local neighborhood interests.

A tiny storefront on the corner of Mulberry and Broome Streets became the headquarters of LIRA. It was there that some young city planners and the men and women of the Italian community discussed and defined, late into the night, the problems and the possible solutions. This vigorous analysis and its recommendations were released less than a year later in the form of a report by the City Planning Commission. The study was called "Little Italy Risorgimento: Proposals for Restoration of an Historic Community." It was this general plan that became the guide and focus for future community actions.

One key problem defined in the report was the need for housing. The existing stock of housing was dilapidated; no new housing or schools had been built in the 125-acre district for sixty years. The Italian community was concerned about the next generation. Housing for young families, particularly for the young men recently returned from the Vietnam War and getting educated on the G.I. Bill, was simply not available. The plan identified small vacant and under-utilized sites for new housing, and pointed out the physical condition of existing buildings to identify units that could be rehabilitated.

The dense area was lacking any green spaces for the residents and was limited to one rundown park, De Salvio Park. The truck traffic from manufacturing uses was in great conflict with pedestrian circulation along Mulberry Street. The traditional, noteworthy buildings and unique storefronts were in danger of falling apart. Another problem that was emphasized was the need for the restoration of the Old Police Headquarters, a graceful building of great architectural merit.

Finally there was the problem of the changing of the pedestrian character of Mulberry Street. The deterioration of the street, due to the increased commercial and vehicular traffic and the condition of the storefronts and building facades, was steadily affecting the businesses in the area.

So when the general goals in the plan were set, the goal of making the three–block stretch of Mulberry Street, with its great concentration of restaurants, into a pedestrian mall, was recognized as a major and most immediate objective of counteracting the neighborhood's decline.

No sooner had the general risorgimento plan been released than it became clear that there was not going to be enough money for the renaissance. The report called for new housing units on several of the vacant sites, for a combined school and housing project on the site of the old P.S. 21, for sprucing up the existing De Salvio Park, and for the conversion of various vacant parcels into parks and piazzas. The Old Police Headquarters, which had just been vacated, needed funds to be transformed into an Italian-American cultural center. In reality, New York City was in the midst of a severe fiscal crisis, so there were no public funds available for the ambitious plans. Thus, the improvement of Mulberry Street and the plan's attendant goal of a weekend closing to dramatize the pleasures of the street became the only immediately implementable part of the overall plan.

Temporary street closing

The closing of Mulberry Street was a test for both the businesses along the street and the planners who participated in the plan. It was done first during one December weekend in 1974, and again during summer weekends in 1975.

When Theo Tarantini, the Health Adminstrator in the area, who became the Executive Director of LIRA, was asked how Mr. Ianello, owner of Umberto's, Mr. Vitale, the florist, the Iuculanos, proprietors of Roma furniture, and Mr. Lepore of Ferrara's got involved in the process, he answered, "They saw themselves as being isolated, sort of what I would say dinosaurs. They said that if Little Italy stopped existing basically, which is what they feared, then there would be no point to having a Roma's or Ferrara's, the most noted Italian bakery in town. They saw the context in which they operated disappearing fast." Mr. Lepore, of Ferrara's, says, "Why build a

Design analysis — storefront activities

Intensity of pedestrians varies from store to store based on the type of business, indicates the needs and opportunities for better planning at any specific location.

Legend:

▦ High intensity

▥ Medium intensity

▨ Low intensity

Design Analysis — Service and Egress

Entrances for movement of goods and people are located. A minimum of 17 feet clear path for emergency vehicles is maintained at all times.

Legend:

Service entrance

Fire egress

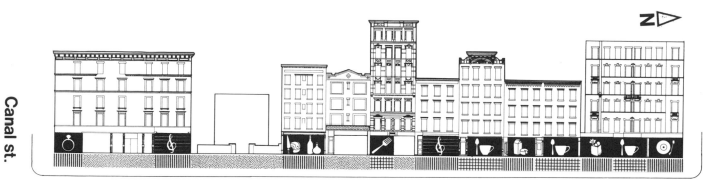

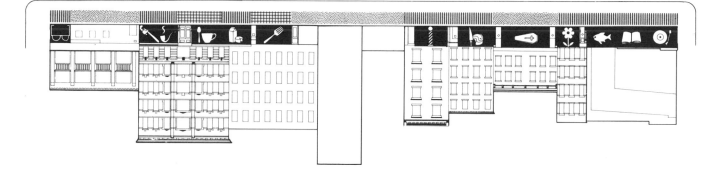

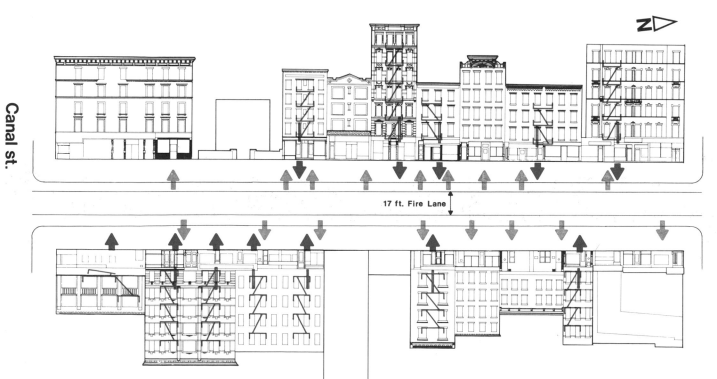

17 ft. Fire Lane

Canal st.

Hester st.

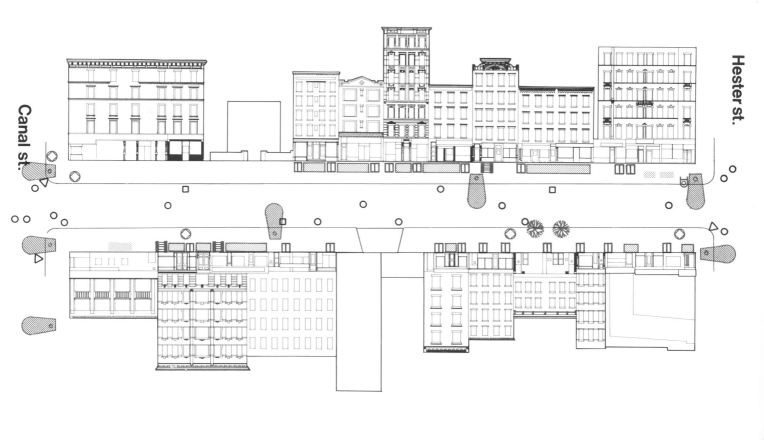

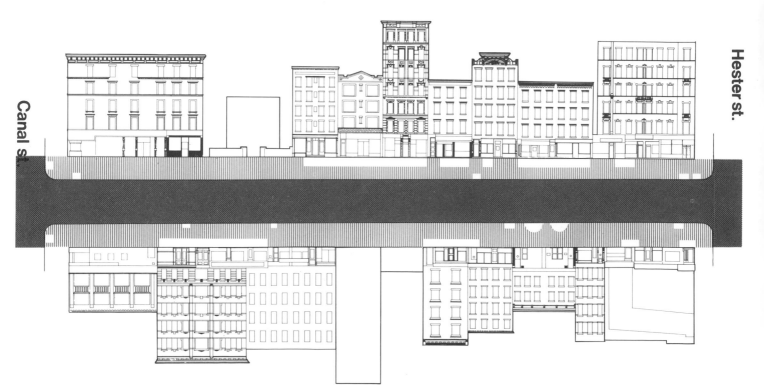

Design Analysis — Street hardware:

Existing functional equipment on the sidewalk is recorded. Through the design process, improvements are planned to work around them or else relocate them.

Legend:

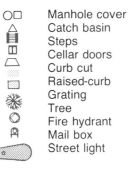

Manhole cover
Catch basin
Steps
Cellar doors
Curb cut
Raised-curb
Grating
Tree
Fire hydrant
Mail box
Street light

Design Analysis — Pedestrian Right of Way:

The entire street, including the roadway is available for pedestrian use, except for area occupied by physical obstruction. Any objects placed along this route must be temporary and movable to allow for emergency vehicles.

Legend:

Street bed

Sidewalk

building or invest in a building or business if nothing is going on around it? Why do it in a vacuum? We could stay for a hundred years. So what, what good would that do? So we want to see a plan if we are going to put our reputations on the line.''

Since the key to the success of any street closing is the support of its business leaders, it became paramount that these local merchants become the pedestrianization committee for Little Italy, and indeed it took a great amount of persuasion and effort to make the owners along the street accept a street closing without the festival. After all, such a measure was only used in Little Italy traditionally for religious processions such as the San Gennaro Festival. It took a lot of adjustments for the community to consent and recognize the importance of these first weekend closings. ''You don't close a street in the City of New York unless there's something significant going on,'' said Mr. Tarantini. And surely the impact of the first closing was dramatic. More importantly, it served as a basis for the future plan.

In analyzing the traffic and pedestrian movement, planners aided by student volunteers had clocked the number of cars and number of people, using the street and surrounding areas, observing traffic flow and counting the number of parking spaces used. What became evident was that most of the cars parked along Mulberry Street before the street closing belonged to the businessmen rather than to tourists and visitors, and that few of the visitors came to the area by car rather than by mass transit. The great opposition to the street closing was from the expensive restaurants that had clientele coming from New Jersey, while the less expensive restaurants welcomed the closing. Unexpected problems surfaced. One example was the case of a businessman who owned a parking lot on Mulberry Street; the community had to find funds to compensate him for the loss of the revenue on those weekends.

One of the first consequences of the closing was the mutual decision by the community and the planners that any pedestrian plan for Mulberry Street had to be limited to weekends, since a permanent mall at that stage in time would limit the daily operations of the industrial and light manufacturing companies remaining on Mulberry Street. Restaurant and tourist related businesses increased by about 20 per cent. The temporary closing stirred interest throughout the city. It was this interest that triggered the community development group LIRA, the Mulberry Street merchants, and the City Planning Commission to launch a more elaborate and permanent pedestrianization plan for a street closing for summer weekends along Mulberry Street.

The design approach: Analysis

Several basic assumptions underlined the planning approach to the Mulberry Street process. First, the street improvements had to be economically within the means of the community. Moreover, they had to be geared for implementation on the basis of self-help and self–maintenance. Community participation therefore became a key issue. The improvements had to be highly visible and completed within a limited amount of time in order to have an immediate visual impact on the neighborhood. The visibility of the project not only creates a general awareness of the physical environment, but becomes an instrument of encouragement, a sign of hope and a signal that good things are happening. Even a small change can have an effect on a rundown community and transform its aesthetic image and the spirit of its people within a matter of weeks or months. Most important, however, was the planners' philosophy that while these improvements were inexpensive, practical, and visible, they were only the beginning of a long process that would stabilize the entire area as a result of a carefully phased plan.

The design approach to the closing of Mulberry Street on the weekends included some of the same design considerations that would apply to a long range street improvement plan. The first step was therefore a thorough analysis of the street's existing conditions and its physical characteristics, recording building elevations to reveal architectural elements, scale, and signage. While elevations show what is outside, an analysis of existing storefront uses shows the activities within; entrances to industrial buildings are seen in contrast to specialty shops and restaurants.

The nature of pedestrian activities and their location was similarly recorded, as was the pattern of vehicular circulation, with major emphasis on servicing commercial buildings, access and egress from delivery docks and the amount of road space required for fire engines to service the street. Based on an up-to-date field survey, the precise location of street hardware was mapped, including all elements located on the sidewalk such as trees, fire hydrants, utilities, stairs, lights, and parking meters.

It soon became evident that some of the analysis applied to almost all other street conditions, such as existing parking issues, service delivery, emergency fire rights-of-way, and existing vacant lots. Typical to Little Italy were the unique storefronts, the distinguished awnings of the family-owned Italian restaurants, the special way the Italians decorated the street in festival time, and the use of their streets as a social meeting place. The in-depth analysis of both common street problems and the specific traits of Little Italy became the general framework for discussion that generated such new and old ideas as the use of the street for art display, bocci courts, market fairs, and lots of fanfare and color along Mulberry Street. In order to be able to record the detail analysis, the designers drew maps and elevations of every building along the street. It was a time-consuming effort, since no record of the buildings was available and they had to rely on photos and visual verification to get a continuous elevation of the street.

The effort paid off. The elevations drawn into all the plans allowed the planners to view the street as a three-dimensional room, thus stressing in their analysis the inter-relationship between the problems along the bed of the street and the buildings themselves, between the activities of the storefronts and the people strolling along the street.

It is hard to define how one creates a sense of partnership and participation between government and the community. How does one explain complex and sometimes dry concepts to a group that faces government with a sense of skepticism and suspicion, and convince them that the professional is not an elitist with a sense of superiority? Anyone who wants a clear answer may find no one

Right: Detail cafe plan
Left: Detail section

Outdoor cafes may encroach the street at specific locations. This cafe accommodates up to thirty two people and provides walking space of five to six feet between the building line and the outdoor cafe.

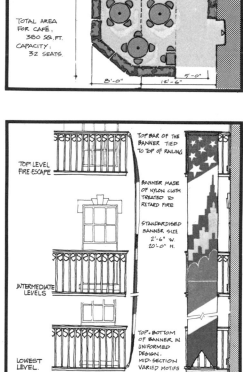

Detail drawings show way of attaching vertical and horizontal banners to building walls, and window sills by fasteners or straps.

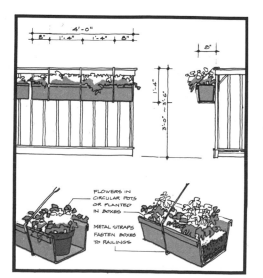

Right: Flowers and planters placed around cafe from pedestrians.

Left: Simple boxes available in the market are placed along window sills and fire escapes as decorative elements.

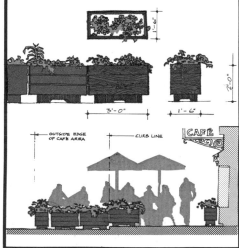

A major alternative is placing sidewalk cafes throughout the bed of the street.

One alternative is to place flowers on fire escapes, windows and along the street. (The community rejected this option because of maintenance costs.)

single reliable answer. But the day the architects presented the community with these realistic drawings of the street, the trust surfaced and the dialogue began. It was the first time that the local people saw vividly what their street looked like in its totality. It gave them a sense of pride. The clean and beautiful line drawings allowed the imagination of everyone to flow and envision how they too could change and improve their own environment.

In a big community meeting in the basement of the Church of the Most Precious Blood on a wintery night, the first analysis drawings were presented to the members of the community. People spilled in from the street, attracted by the drawings that covered the entire walls of the room. The analysis drawings presented at this meeting were: a perspective of the street and its sidewalk, emphasizing the location and space available to extend commercial uses into the street; a perspective of the street as a three-

dimensional space, with a detailed elevation showing architectural details, window signs, fire escapes, awnings, and all elements of future potential to strengthen the existing image of the street; a map showing emergency deliveries, fire-engine routes, and other service requirements to be used in the event of the weekend closing; and a plan depicting the areas within vacant lots and areas next to blank buildings that could be utilized for various recreational community uses.

Presenting design alternatives

Anxious to get everyone in the community involved in the design process, the planners had prepared simplified colored perspective drawings. These drawings expressed the contents of the proposed closing and showed what the street would feel and look like and the atmosphere that would be created after the improvements were made. Various alternatives for the new image of

In this alternative, banners are hung on fire escapes to unify the street's image. This option was enthusiastically endorsed.

Another alternative is to string banners across the street at intersections defining the blocks. Community approved two entrance banners.

the street were presented. It is only with such data and such drawings firmly in hand that the Mulberry Street mall could seriously be discussed and the details of its implementation refined.

The community members loved the outdoor cafe drawing, which showed the restaurants along the street extended onto the sidewalk. This night-scene drawing was filled with umbrellas, tables, chairs, awnings — and lots of people. One of the design options presented was that of transforming the whole street into an urban hanging garden, with plenty of flowers on window sills, in doorways, along fire escapes, and along the sidewalk. Another design option for the street was attaching banners horizontally across Mulberry Street, from building to building, creating a festive continuous "ceiling" above the shop activity below. The most popular option presented was that of hanging vertical banners from the fire escape along the street. It was attractive to the community that every banner could be designed

to celebrate an Italian restaurant or association, or other group with a strong affinity for the Italian cultural spirit.

These beautiful drawings were presented to the community by Patrick Ping-Tze Too, the project urban designer of Chinese origin. Viewed a little bit with suspicion at the beginning of the meeting, he was applauded as the drawings were presented. Patrick became the key architect and the confidant of the Little Italy community.

A dialogue with the community

And at this crucial stage of the project the concepts and their implicit themes were modified. Alternatives for outdoor cafe layouts were supplied by the city designers, including different seating arrangements, specifying distances between tables, ways of placing umbrellas, and details of wooden platforms to elevate the roadbed to sidewalk level. With such diagrams to assist them,

From left to right clockwise:

A mural by Richard Hass on a blank wall.

Noteworthy buildings exhibit draws curiosity and pride.

Entrance banners at both ends of the mall.

The Urban Design Group banner salutes the community.

Vertical banners represent Italian Institutions and local groups.

Little Italy at night, after improvements.

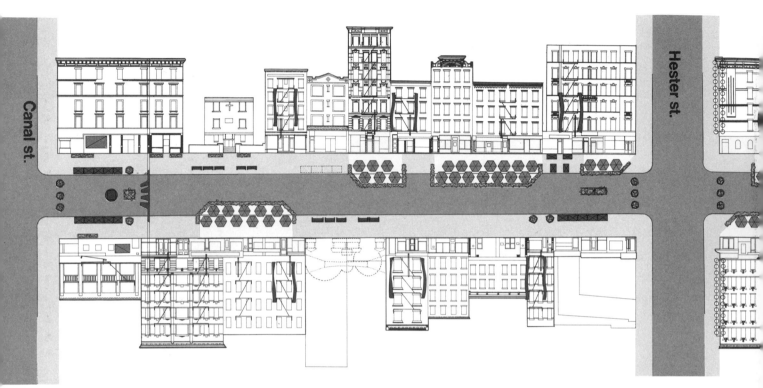

owners could arrange their umbrella-bedecked tables in a number of different configurations within their allocated areas along the sidewalks.

The designers showed various ideas for arranging flowers, even to the point of embellishing the police barricades that would be set out to define the mall and defend it from careless drivers. Most of the owners agreed that flowers would be used to brighten up the street, but not to the extent of turning Mulberry Street into a greenhouse. Members of the community pointed out the expense of maintenance requirements for floral decorations on every fire escape and window. It was decided that flowers would be contained in redwood planters along the street itself. For the sake of efficiency, planters on wheels would be used instead of public barricades for the weekend

closings, while on weekdays they could be rolled over to decorate the sidewalks.

Of all the basic concepts, the banners were most enthusiastically received by the community —but only the vertical ones. Horizontal banners, it was pointed out, would get in the way of the decorations for the famous street festivals. They also looked too much like the banners used in Chinatown next door. At the suggestion of Antonio Morello, a new element was introduced into the plan in the form of two major entrance banners, which became the gateways to the three-block mall at both entrances. The entrance banners were 25 feet by 25 feet and were made out of a fishing net transparent enough to keep the view of the Empire State Building, which could be seen at a distance. An Italian emblem with lions was above a sign which said "Little Italy Benvenuti."

The vertical banners, the design of which was jointly decided on by the community and the Urban Design Group, had a firmament of stars running across the top, with the colors of the Italian flag running across the bottom. In the central white area of each were scattered the assorted symbols, logos, and insignias of local organizations and businesses. The Urban Design Group originally entertained a hope that the banners would be sewn or embroidered by local women in the community. Actually, however, Antonio Morello and Donato Savoie, designers who lived in the area and were very active in the neighborhood, designed most of the banners, except for one or two that were created by the Urban Design Group.

A final plan evolves

The final plan evolved after the different analysis maps were superimposed over each other. The hardware and service maps, which reflected areas needed for ambulances and fire trucks, were superimposed with a map that presented the desired improvements. Thus the sidewalk space that was freed for the use of sidewalk cafes and stalls was delineated to avoid conflict with existing street furniture or with needed entry and delivery areas. The location of street furniture, the rolling planters, and information kiosk, and the plan for hanging the banners were also included. Final plans were also suggested for converting some of the vacant lots along the street into recreation areas; one, it was suggested, could become a bocci court, another converted into a small market fair.

Individual buildings were selected for cleaning and painting, an urgent need in this community. Others with blank walls were earmarked as large canvasses for artwork with the help of a civic group called Citywalls. Richard Haas, a well-known painter, was asked to paint storefront images on existing austere walls to give the illusion of street continuity. The blank wall at the Canal Street entrance to the mall was selected to become the location for a photographic exhibit of noteworthy buildings. Thus it was not only the

Above: Il Cortile, a restaurant re-born (designed by Morello and Savoie).

Below: A day scene along Mulberry Street.

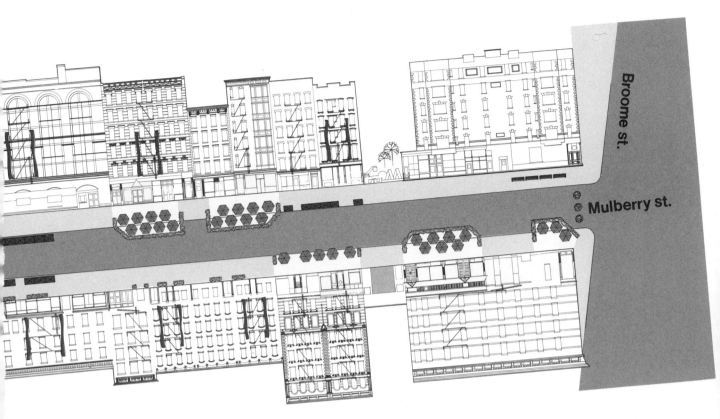

Overleaf: This banner represents the
Rockefeller Family Fund, who gave seed
money for the project.

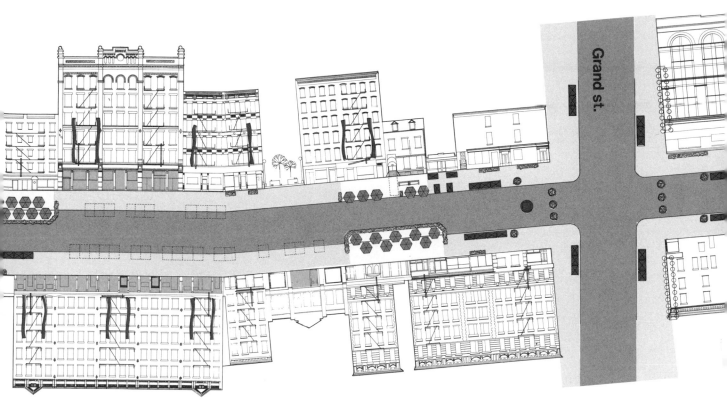

Grand st.

The final plan

Legend:

- Seating
- Planters
- Banners
- Sidewalk cafe
- Restaurant
- Vendors
- Kiosk
- Artwork
- Exhibit

occasion of the street closing itself that spurred what has been heralded as a *risorgimento*, it was what the occasion allowed people to see, in many cases for the first time, about the assets of the overall environment.

Roles of implementation

As the implementation stage proceeded, the community and the planners agreed as to the importance of three basic guidelines:

• To close the street on weekends for pedestrian uses without handicapping the essential services. This was achieved by leaving seventeen feet clear for emergency vehicles and by closing the street at given hours.

• To improve Mulberry Street with some defined framework without prohibiting individual expressions. This was achieved by specifying certain elements with size, location, and colors, and yet allowing participants to freely express their characters within that framework.

• To allow flexibility for implementation. This was achieved by defining the roles of the community and government and allowing neighborhoods to make improvements according to their ability.

Throughout the preparation of the final plan, implementation tasks were defined. Roles were set as to the responsibilities of the government planners and those assigned to community groups. The Urban Design Group was formally responsible for the development of the final design, the coordination of its implementation with both other city agencies and private manufacturers, and the provision of a detailed budget for the improvements. LIRA (this coalition of nongovernmental interests was the Urban Design Group's "client") was responsible for getting permits for the street closing and receiving owners' permission for hanging banners, for lighting installation, and for the coordination of sidewalk cafe owners with the puppet show, antique fair, and other street activities. LIRA would coordinate publicity, provide live entertainment for opening night, and arrange for sanitation pickups, which would be increased during the weekend hours. It was also responsible for enlisting community support to clean vacant lots, to maintain the mall, and se-

curing the required funding for banners and street furniture. As it turned out, the Urban Design Group played a more major role than anticipated in the Mulberry Street implementation stage.

The planners investigated in great detail every element of materials, cost of design, installation cost, method of lighting, and quantities required. For instance, the planners evaluated the advantages of nylon banners as compared to cotton or burlap ones. Similar information was gathered on planters, flowers, trees, and umbrellas. At least three purchasing manufacturers were approached for each item.

Most of the implementation stage, however, took place in the field itself, where Susan Orsini, the designer in charge of implementing the project, presented alternative items to every merchant as she was walking down Mulberry Street. In describing that stage of community participation, she says, "on one hand the people wanted to take complete charge of implementing the mall, and on the other hand they wanted us to do everything for them." It soon became clear that the responsibilities of government and community were overlapping.

While the role of raising funds was originally LIRA's, it was the city planners' presentation of their drawings that secured the commitment of $25,000 from the Rockefeller Family Fund. When it came to increasing the number of banners, jointly with LIRA, they went from door to door to get businesses to purchase sixty banners for the opening celebration. The Rockefeller Family Fund grant encouraged businesses to pitch in, donate additional banners, and to negotiate with suppliers to provide new street furniture needed to maximize the visibility of the improvements.

It had been estimated that improvements associated with the mall would come to around $30,000. Besides the Rockefeller Family Fund, the money was donated by neighborhood banks, businesses, and the residents themselves. The total sum covered the manufacturing and installation of the banners, lighting the street, and the purchase of the redwood planters. These funds also paid for high school students to refinish the wall in preparation for the architectural photo exhibit. The community, with funding from

Citywalls, was able to hire the artist to paint murals on two other building walls. Inspired by the support of the local businessmen, major Italian businesses, including Alitalia, agreed to buy fifteen additional banners.

Economic impact: The street today

On July 30, 1975, after a small ceremony to light the banners, the mall opened. It was a tremendous success. Theo Tarantini, in his description of the event, said: "Every table and chair that was available was out on the street, and I thought it was a miracle. It was as if you were in Rome's Piazza Navona. The umbrellas were up, there was music. I felt like crying for joy. Finally, all the work was paying off. It was as if nobody had ever seen a car before and did not care to see another car again."

The streets around Mulberry Street were jammed. It was hard to tell where one restaurant ended and one began. The severe-looking Italian women of the community, wearing black, were sitting in their chairs, looking with pride at the thousands of people who came to celebrate the beginning of *risorgimento*. Television reporters covered the event extensively. Did they realize that this event was the result of six months' extensive work by a dedicated community? The vertical banners, hanging from the fire escapes, added to the festivity of the street.

What happened in 1975, and the momentum building since, adds up to a lot more than a bunch of banners, though. What happened on Mulberry Street was not just window dressing. It was the creation of a catalyst that directed community energy and civic pride into gradual economic stability, longer-range physical improvements, and a spiritual rejuvenation of the whole neighborhood. Most of the banners have worn out, but the new landscape maintenance programs are underway. Fifteen new restaurants have opened since, and the facades of almost a dozen existing ones have been renovated, others painted and cleaned. For the first time in sixty years, storefront activity is booming.

At the time of the city's worst budgetary crisis, when development was at a halt and businesses were going bankrupt all over the city, federal government and banks were impressed by the unique energy and activity generated in Little Italy; they decided to provide loans to new businesses and restaurants. Private investors followed the lead and put their hard-earned savings into building restaurants, such as the successful renovation of Il Cortile.

Describing the success of the Mulberry Street Mall, the present president of LIRA and the owner of Umberto's Clam House, Oscar Ianello, said: "The community somehow remained intact, despite the lack of city resources. You see a wine and cheese store opening and you think of a few years ago when stores were closing. You see another well-designed quality restaurant; a new installed cafe, and it makes you walk down Mulberry Street with pride."

Shortly after the mall opening, the government planners and the community jointly put forward a plan for the Special District of Little Italy, ensuring the future protection of the neighborhood's integrity, adding to the stability of the whole area. New housing and the rehabilitation of the Old Police Headquarters are still in planning stages.

Through its rebuilding and revitalization Little Italy will prosper, yet maintain its myth, mystery, and memory.

Noteworthy buildings:

Top left:
The Old Police Headquarters

Top right:
St. Patricks Church

Bottom Left:
149 Mulberry Street

Bottom right:
375 Broome Street

PRESERVATION BECOMES THE LAW

Little Italy Zoning District

The community was elated by the success of its revitalization plan. It was united for the first time, and it had the ability to reach government on a personal level. Having a real stake in their neighborhood, the people became determined to protect the area and were adamant about developing a more far-reaching plan to insure the character of Little Italy. Clearly, the people of Little Italy were confident in the stability of their area and were ready to work for its future.

Before the designation to a special zoning district, the Little Italy zoning permitted high-rise tower development, as well as encouraging manufacturing and parking uses. Such development would certainly conflict with the community efforts of maintaining the unique neighborhood quality of Little Italy, and disrupt the continuity of the street at ground level. The result would defeat the major objectives of the revitalization efforts. The second stage therefore was focused on proposing zoning legislation to create a framework to strengthen and preserve the physical character of the neighborhood, with emphasis placed on the quality of the street. The legislation includes guidelines that insure a relationship of new building to the scale of the existing buildings of the neighborhood, and creates measures to promote the economic stability and vitality in the area.

These goals were well expressed in the Special Little Italy District Legislation proposal:

● To preserve and strengthen the historical and cultural character of the community of Little Italy;

● To protect the scale of the storefronts and the character of the existing retail use along Mulberry Street and other major shopping streets so that Little Italy will remain as a unique regional shopping area, and thereby strengthen the economic base of the city;

● To preserve the vitality of street life by reducing conflict between pedestrian and vehicular traffic;

● To permit rehabilitation and new development

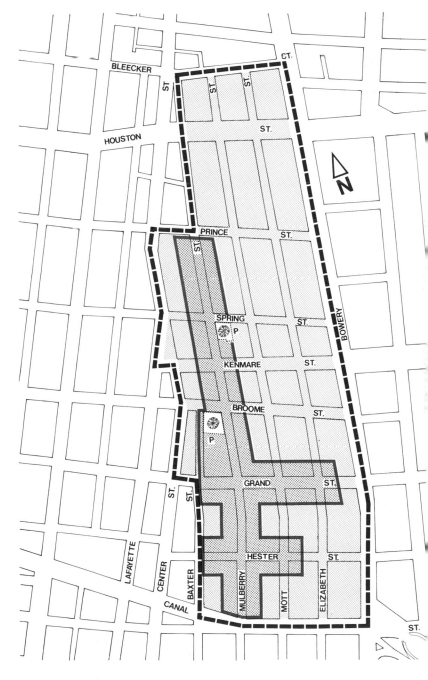

The Special District Plan

Preservation Area

Mulberry Street Retail Spine

✳ **P** Parks

▬ ▬ District Boundary

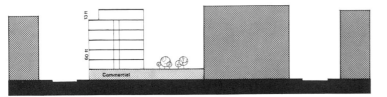

INTERIOR LOT SECTION

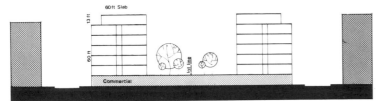

THROUGH BLOCK SECTION

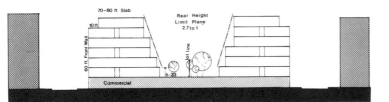

THROUGH BLOCK ALTERNATIVE

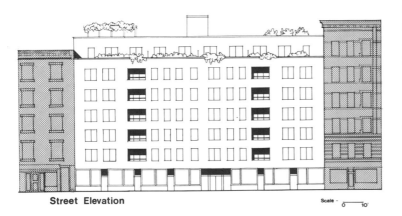

Street Elevation

Scale - 0 — 10'

Design controls for the Mulberry Street Spine: Regional character is reinforced by mandating retail stores at ground level and by creating storefront guidelines; residential controls limit building heights to relate to the existing scale of Little Italy.

consistent with the residential character and scale of the existing buildings in the area;

● To provide amenities such as public space and street trees to improve the physical environment;

● To discourage the demolition of noteworthy buildings that are significant to the character of the area;

● To promote the more desirable use of land in the area and thus to preserve the value of land and buildings, and thereby protect and strengthen the city's tax revenues, consistent with the foregoing purposes.

Subareas within the district

While the first stages of Little Italy revitalization were concentrated on Mulberry Street, the special district includes the larger borders of the immediate impact area. The district includes three different subareas, each with unique characteristics that form the basis for design guidelines. The preservation area is mainly residential, two peripheral corridors are areas of truck concentration and manufacturing, and the Mulberry Street spine is a retail, restaurant, and tourist center.

The Preservation Area: This area consists of residential buildings, streets where shopping and socializing occur, where children play and the elderly gather in front of buildings to sun themselves on a fine day. The tree-lined narrow streets and the low buildings are conducive to a friendly, relaxed sense of community. The area contains a network of small stores, a variety of institutions, schools, health facilities, and churches.

In recognizing the narrowness of the streets, the Special District mandates a limitation of the building heights to seven stories, setback at the sixth-story level. The guidelines allow 60 per cent to 70 per cent coverage of the building on the lot. Open space is developed in backyards and rooftops. In order to insure the continuity of the street walls, new developments have to comply with the existing street wall both in height and character. Limited recesses, such as bay windows, are permitted in order to allow flexibility in design. The guidelines mandate transparency on ground floor. This means opening the ground level with doors or windows, in order to prevent blank walls along the street and to enhance the pedestrian experience. In cases where blank walls of twenty feet or more exist, artwork or greenery must be provided. The masonry material typical of the area is mandated throughout Little Italy.

Tree plantings at intervals of twenty-five feet of streetfront are mandated along new and renovated buildings. The trees of a minimum of three-and-one-half-inch diameter are to be planted flush to grade and to be maintained by the owner.

Every effort is made to discourage parking. A special permit from the City Planning Commission is required, and notification to authorities should demonstrate that there are insufficient parking spaces in the vicinity and that such parking will not contribute to serious traffic congestions in the area.

The Corridors: The periphery of the area, called corridors, are two areas that loop around the preservation area and function primarily as traffic channels. They are lined with manufacturing and industrial buildings. It is within these boundaries that parking and curb cuts are permitted.

The Mulberry Street spine: The urban design guidelines for the Mulberry Street Spine place restrictions on heights and coverage of buildings, in addition to seeking the reinforcement of regional activities along the street by mandating retail stores on a ground level and by creating guidelines for storefronts. In order to encourage the continuance of retail activity along the street, 100-per-cent coverage of the building on ground level allows restaurants to expand. The retail activity on the ground level is mandated in all new and renovated buildings. Both have to provide new brick-paved sidewalks with granite curbs along the edges. The design is left to the discretion of the owner, while the curb unifies the street.

To strengthen the retail activity along the spine and ensure the continuity of street activities, a special list containing stores and commercial activities called the Little Italy Use Group is established. This list applies to the Mulberry Street spine and encourages all new land uses to maintain the unique and intimate retail character of the area. It prohibits incompatible uses, such as large

Existing typical storefronts.

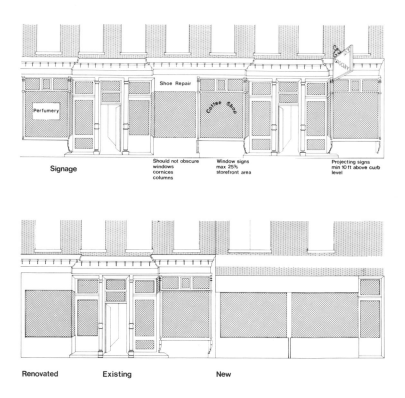

Top drawing: Typical elevations of an historic storefront.

Bottom drawing: New design guidelines are inspired by existing storefronts, but allow for modern design.

parking structures, major department stores, or banks. Categories under use groups include convenience retail establishments, such as bakeries, drugstores, and restaurants, and retail or service establishments, such as bookstores, newsstands, and craft shops.

To preserve the original storefront materials and scale and to relate new storefronts to existing ones along the street, the Special District encourages the development of small stores and includes sign regulations. Storefront regulations are:
● Show windows shall have a sill height of not more than 2'6" above curb level and extend to a maximum height between 8'0" and 10'0" above curb level;
● The storefront shall have transparent areas no more than 10'0" in width, measured horizontally, and shall be separated by a divider of no less than 6" in width;
● Storefront entrance doors shall be set back a minimum of 2'0" behind the vertical surface of the show windows.

The following regulations apply to all signs:
● Accessory business signs may not occupy more than 25 per cent of the total area of the storefront, measured from curb level to 10'0" above curb level;
● All permitted signs that project from the front building wall shall be located not less than 10'0" above curb level;
● Accessory business signs may not cover columns, cornices, or sills.

The Mulberry Street spine area also limits the heights of buildings to seven stories, setting setback level at the six-story level, permitting sunlight to penetrate to the street. Special front wall regulations mandate buildings to be built to the street, recesses are permitted for individual expression, and transparency and treatment of ground level blank walls are required as in the preservation area. However, because of the pedestrian concentration along Mulberry Street, no trees are mandated and no parking or curb cuts are allowed.

Two years after the revitalization of the street, the Special Little Italy District had become a law. It was a result of many hours of presentations to the community, and a variety of public hearings. During the process, the District had undergone several changes due to input from neighboring communities. For example, the original provision that encouraged horizontal signs on storefronts typical in Little Italy was eliminated because the neighboring Chinese community found it too restrictive. Limiting the use on storefronts of materials such as plastic, stainless steel, aluminum, or porcelain and enamel on steel was considered to be subjective and too restrictive by the Planning Commission and was therefore eliminated in the final draft.

The Little Italy Preservation District has become a prototype for other communities to create guidelines for the preservation of neighborhoods.

A New Plan for the Old Police Headquarters

The cultural committee headed by Louise Nevelson and Jacqueline Onassis, jointly with Little Italy Restoration Association, developed a plan to reuse the building as a cultural center. The adjoining open space is planned as an urban plaza to link Mulberry Street Mall with the building. The buildings along center Market Place, facing the building, and the cultural center will be renovated and improved. The Old Police Headquarters is both designated as a landmark and is on the National Register of historic buildings.

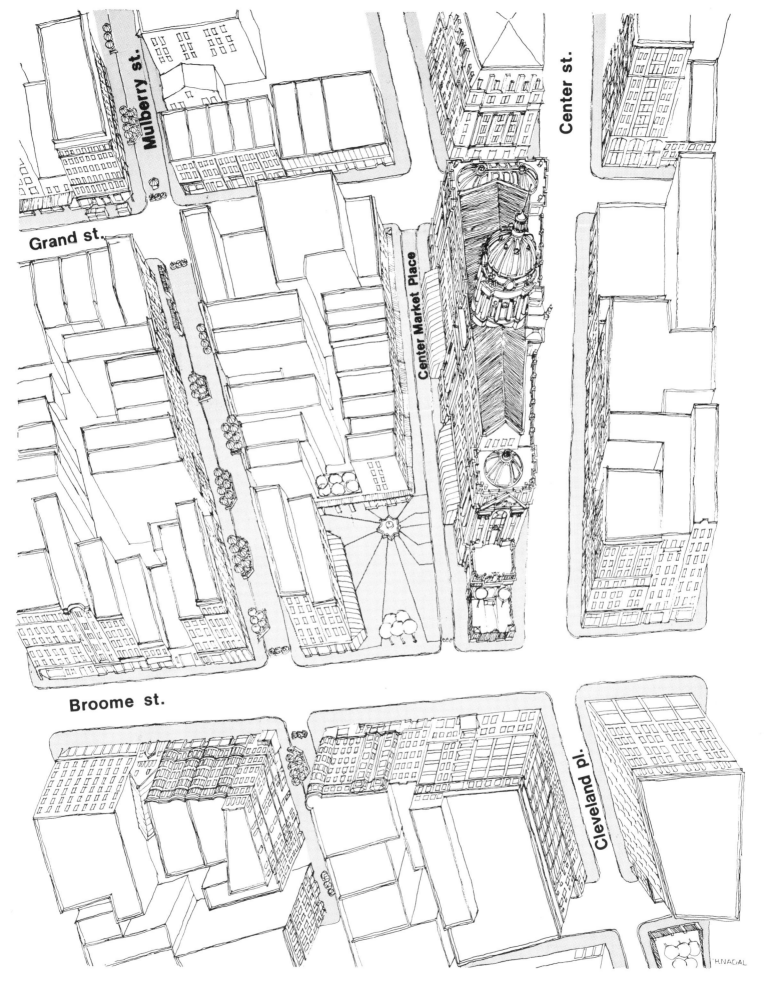

Mulberry st.

Center st.

Grand st.

Center Market Place

Broome st.

Cleveland pl.

H. NADAL

Birds-eye view of Newkirk Plaza before improvement.

NEWKIRK PLAZA IN BROOKLYN

Newkirk Plaza, in Brooklyn, New York, is not a typical street. Newkirk is actually a deck, turned street. Four hundred feet long, it runs above a subway station. Thirty-four shops line the deck on both sides, with their service entrances facing the side streets behind.

Yet Newkirk *is* typical as a street in a very important sense. It is small scale, a retail center located in a residential neighborhood where moderate income levels have been able to sustain local trade through the years. It has survived competition from large shopping centers and maintained the personal quality of a neighborhood shopping street. The problems and potential of Newkirk Plaza are similar to those of other neighborhoods around the country.

Newkirk Plaza, as we know it today, was developed at the turn of the century. Newkirk Avenue had been a station on the Brooklyn Heights Railroad, whose ground level tracks intersected with the cross streets in its path. As the residential area grew, these on-grade crossings became dangerous. In 1903, the state approved funds for relocating the tracks below ground and for putting bridges above the crossings; by 1908, the present Newkirk deck was finished.

So Newkirk, almost 70 years old, was a mall long before the recent craze for creating malls. In fact, Newkirk had everything required for a suc-

cessful street-saving process. It had an economic base with active patrons. Its architecture was hardly what you would call significant, but the buildings along both sides of the plaza had a certain modest charm, visual continuity, scale and style. While the street attracted a large number of pedestrians, there weren't any cars. An excellent opportunity for planning a street for people.

Newkirk, located in the North Flatbush area of Brooklyn, not only catered to several small surrounding neighborhoods, but its shops also had no competition from any other retail area within a ten minute walk. Flatbush Avenue, for example, the main shopping spine in Brooklyn, is eight blocks away.

The plaza runs north and south at street level. Over the shops, facing the plaza on both sides, are two and three story apartment buildings. Entrances to the apartments and delivery entrances for the shops are located on the side streets, East 16th Street and Marlborough Road.

The area is served by buses, in addition to the subway. To reach or leave the subway below, you go through a station house, situated in the center of the plaza; this station house, bridging a long open airshaft above the tracks, gives the deck an H-shaped configuration.

Newkirk is mostly middle and upper-middle class, distinctly family oriented, with private

Below: Structure in the center is the subway station house; stairs lead to the train platforms below the open cut. Stores link the deck forming a vehicle-free plaza.

Marlborough St.   Newkirk Plaza   Apts.   Stores   Apts.   Stores   E. 16 th. St.

homes as well as low and high rise apartment buildings. Moderate and low income families have begun moving into the area in recent years, adding to its ethnic and economic diversity. Besides young couples with children, there is a sizeable population of elderly people.

When the Urban Design Group got involved, upon the request of the local Brooklyn planning office, discussions with the community began. Both old-timers and newcomers voiced concern about Newkirk Plaza's declining image and deteriorating physical condition.

Getting the community involved

It was this community concern that had led to several plans for Newkirk Plaza's revitalization through the years. Myriad studies were done. A local architect came up with an elaborate $3 million design proposal to cover the entire plaza with a roof structure. If anybody had been able to raise that much funding, there would have been no reason for the Urban Design Group to become involved. All of the earlier plans had common faults: impossible grandeur, plans that could not

Housing types in the vicinity of the plaza include single homes and high rise apartments.

be handled in phases and therefore could not be implemented by the community, or plans that plainly lacked the inspiration to generate community participation.

Since several previous attempts at planning for Newkirk Plaza had failed, the designers felt that the best way to gain the confidence of the community was to present a plan that had already been a success elsewhere. They therefore presented the process for the revitalization of Mulberry Street in Little Italy, which was feasible and involved community action.

The Mulberry Street presentation was made in a bank on the plaza to members of the Flatbush Development Corporation, local merchants, and a number of community representatives. Recognizing that the plan for Little Italy had realistic goals and a modest budget, the community became enthusiastic about the prospects for their own street.

Community involvement often comes about through the efforts of a strong local leader, and that was the case in Newkirk. In this initial meeting a young leader emerged, Michael Weiss, a high school teacher in his thirties. He became a rallying point for all, and the single person to depend on to follow through on details.

A healthy economic base

As you recall, the approach to street revitalization efforts requires that there be a healthy economic base and to start, Newkirk had a solid base. No one was throwing up their hands in resignation; no one was declaring economic or social bankruptcy.

What was Newkirk's strength? Every day, some 14,000 commuters passed through the plaza en route to the subway. The shops—ranging from groceries and pharmacies to florists and restaurants—were bustling with activity. There was even a long waiting list for merchants wanting to rent stores along the plaza. Furthermore, Newkirk Plaza is a physical phenomenon in New York, and would be one most anywhere: a true mall, free of cars, where people can meet their friends, walk their babies, and buy a loaf of bread.

But after seventy years as a retail hub, the plaza had gradually become rundown, and in

14,000 people use the subway daily. There is little except the stores to keep them there for some length of time.

Chain-link fence surround the open cut. The train is barely visible but the noise is heard throughout the day.

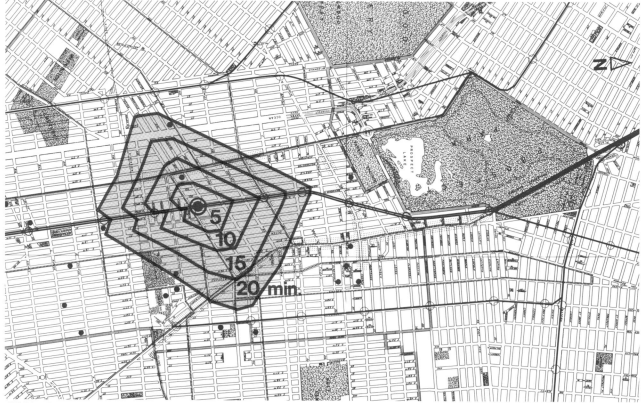

Within the pedestrian catchment areas of Newkirk Plaza
—a walking distance of five to twenty minutes—the
Plaza is the sole open public space.

spots, it bordered on dilapidation. This was the
state of affairs the community was anxious to
turn around.

The match between the professional designers
and planners from the city and the community occurred when the word spread among the Newkirk
merchants about the successful work in Little
Italy. Simultaneously it became clear that there
was a community in Brooklyn ready to launch a
street improvement project.

Merchants and shoppers

To acquaint themselves with the area, the designers spent ten days in the field observing the
movement of people, photographing the buildings, and collecting first impressions of the major
planning issues of the area. One of the first things
they did was to go into the stores and talk to the
owners and to the shoppers. Among others, the
designers spoke to the owner of Grillo's, a seafood restaurant connected to a seafood store.
There since 1930 and intending to expand, Grillo's was an obvious ally. Then there was Edward
Fox, who owns Lipton's Pharmacy, which had
been in existence as long as the plaza.

Other, more formal meetings with the Newkirk
Plaza Merchants Association and members of
Community Planning Board 14 followed. The
approach to revitalization was described and a decision was made to form a task force, the Newkirk Plaza Task Force. This was to become a
closely knit team that represented all groups, including the Urban Design Group, other planners
of the Brooklyn City Planning Department, and
the Flatbush Development Corporation, whose
leaders coordinated and chaired the task force's
meetings.

The prime responsibility of the task force was to propose a plan that could be handled without major amounts of capital but that would produce well designed, highly visible improvements. At the same time, the task force was able to supply the design group with constant feedback from the community. As it evolved, it functioned in several ways: organizing meetings between the community representatives and the planners; raising funds both from the community and from outside resources. It was this well defined organization that was to become the "client" in Newkirk.

Studying the impact area

Getting to know Newkirk Plaza meant also getting to know the surrounding areas. The designers got data from city maps, transportation maps, census tracts, and from the earlier planning studies for the plaza.

The maps of the area identified the primary, secondary, and local streets, the residential and commercial districts, schools, parks, bridges, railroad tracks, and major open spaces.

The Transit Authority and the Traffic Department supplied other studies, and these gave the locations of subway stations, bus routes, and an approximation of the number of pedestrians generated by subways and buses. The design team plotted Newkirk's surrounding neighborhoods within a five to twenty minute walk from the plaza to see what services and open spaces were available to the pedestrian. The data confirmed that *no* significant retail concentration or public open space was within one half mile of Newkirk, and therefore, the plaza's position, not only as a major shopping center, but also as a potential source for recreation, was essential.

Once it was known how far people were accustomed to travel in order to shop at Newkirk, the designers went on to learn who came to Newkirk and what their needs were. Previous planning studies provided a general history of the area, census tracts showed the composition of the neighborhoods, the range of income, and the age distribution. The large concentration of elderly people in the area influenced decisions about such things as seating and rest areas within the plaza proper.

The street proper

The collection of more detailed data followed the first stage of the neighborhood study. It was then that observation, conservation, and photographic fieldwork became necessary.

Questionnaires were sent around to the community and merchants, asking them for input regarding major problems in the area. Through observation, the physical condition of the buildings edging the plaza was evaluated, identifying which ones needed cleaning, repairing, renovation or restoration. Knowing the various owners was useful in seeking support for projected improvements of private property, and in establishing levels of responsibility for maintenance.

The designers then made elevation drawings of the building facades on the plaza, showing their impact on scale, architectural character, store fronts, and signs. Photographs were taken of each building, then put together to make one long photograph; that composite was translated into the drawings. This is an important stage, because all the elements that can influence a proposal—from grade to copings, from signs to cornice lines—are emphasized on these elevations and express the character and detail of the street's "walls." This elevation of the street facade in its entirety is a view that people rarely get.

Meanwhile, the questionnaires started coming in, pointing up the issues that were on the minds of the merchants, and confirming earlier observations. The questionnaire results were combined with the data collected in the field. All this information was then recorded on base maps, at different scales. The smallest scale showed the overall area; the larger scale maps showed such details as fire hydrants, lamp posts, and service entrances.

An issues and problems map evolved as a result of the surveys, questionnaires, drawings, and photographs. This map illustrated and emphasized the physical improvements most needed. The subway platform and station house were in great need of restoration. The station house needed improvements, inside and out. The Transit Authority surveyed and recorded the damage and structural weaknesses of the plaza deck and its parapets. Everyone knew that there was a plaza

Merchandise is displayed on the Plaza.

Check-cashing store and market stand side-by-side.

upstairs and a subway downstairs, but the experience of connections and movements occurring from level to level — the sounds, the various views, the contrast between retail life above and the platform life down below was not appreciated. People had been accustomed to perceiving them separately, rather than as one. To dramatize this point, a cut away drawing of a section of the plaza was made, including the stores, deck, station house, and subway, from top to bottom. This was a multiuse complex, an urban village in miniature.

For understanding the circulation systems, pedestrian and vehicular, the information about traffic direction, signals, and parking was recorded to show how Newkirk is influenced by motorists. As it turned out, the most common kind of street conflict — that between pedestrians and cars — was virtually absent.

Studying where people generally congregated while passing through the plaza pointed up areas where seating and conveniences were most needed. For example, the west side of the plaza does not go straight through the block, from Foster to Newkirk Avenue, as the east side does. Pedestrian circulation on the east was extraordi-

Traffic and circulation.

Circulation throughout the plaza is used exclusively by pedestrians, while the adjoining streets carry vehicular traffic. Metered parking spaces are located along sidewalk curbs around the plaza.

Legend:

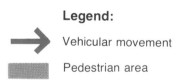

Vehicular movement

Pedestrian area

The Plaza during a summer fair.

Outdoor display creates a mall effect.

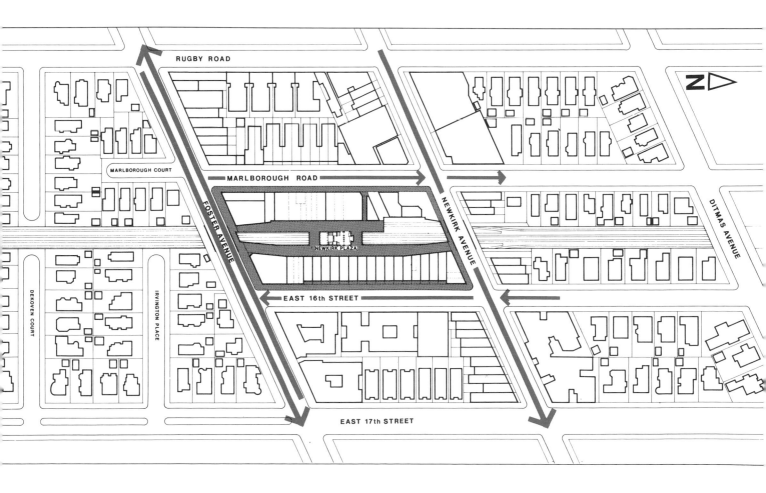

West Elevation

narily busy — with a lot of people bumping into each other. There was also considerable congestion at the station house during rush hours, because some of the doors were locked for security reasons. Other vehicular conflicts occurred outside the plaza; for example, congestion at the service station at the corner of Marlborough Road. Such conflicts had to be known before gearing up for a change.

The easterly edge of the plaza, because of its direct access to the major avenues, clearly had the highest volume of shoppers. In the analysis of the retail storefronts lining Newkirk, detailed notes were made about the type, names, hours and delivery schedules of every store. This retail information enabled the designers to understand the varying levels of pedestrian traffic and the mix of activities generated, thus determining what kinds of amenities and improvements might be added. In contrast, the westerly edge, with less direct access, had a noticeably lower volume of people.

Hardware had to be taken into consideration for the planning process, and so every physical object within and around the plaza was charted and recorded on a map. The map eventually served to determine the effect of the existing street furniture (lights, gratings, awnings, and fences) on the pedestrian circulation. It was thus possible to tell where existing hardware might be relocated, if required. This map also demonstrated the areas that were now available for introducing new hardware, such as lights and benches.

Activities.

This map shows the types of stores and intensity of pedestrians activities generated by each store. Blank walls break the continuity of activities.

Typical storefronts on the Plaza

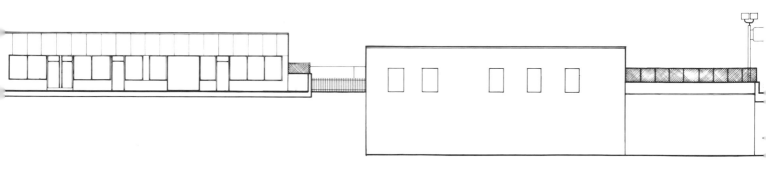

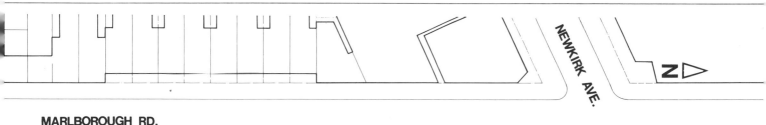

MARLBOROUGH RD.

NEWKIRK AVE.

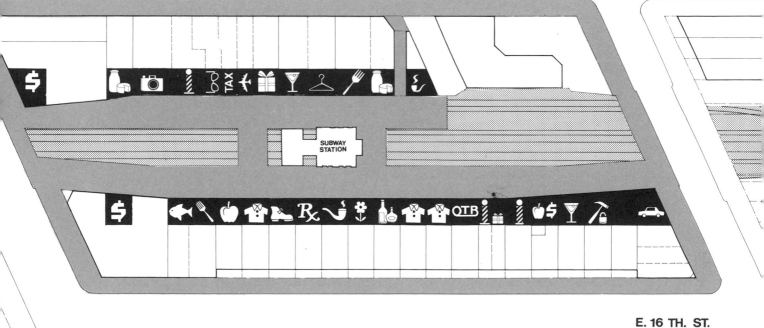

SUBWAY STATION

E. 16 TH. ST.

FOSTER AVE.

East Elevation

The beginning of a plan

This initial phase—the collection, mapping, and analysis of data—took about five weeks, with about one and a half people putting in full time. The material was then presented to the community. At this presentation, community groups and the planners agreed on several key points that were eventually worked into the design proposal.

It became clear that while Newkirk Plaza's physical layout was ideal, offering a rich mix of services and activities in close proximity, it was functioning quite a bit below its potential, not only as a shopping center, but also as a focus of neighborhood events.

To begin with, the plaza lacked the kinds of physical amenities that make a street comfortable for shopping and conducive to friendly encounters. Even though it was the only "open space" in the vicinity, pedestrian amenities had never been integrated into the plaza's plan. The community was beginning to see that Newkirk had all the makings of an open air marketplace.

Also, the revitalization plan indicated the need for a unified image requiring a highly visible design treatment, yet within a manageable budget.

Finally, the improved plaza would serve, not only local residents and merchants, but also as an attraction to the Flatbush community as a whole. With growing confidence in the area's long term stability, more private investment would gradually follow.

Hardware

Street furnishings, service and shop entrances are noted along the side street and the Plaza.

Legend:

- ◎ Lighting fixture
- ◈ Fire hydrant
- ▣ Public telephone booth
- o— Parking meter
- ⊂ Street light
- ◫ Cellar doors
- ∞ Trash area
- ⏢ Awning
- △ Entrance
- ☰ Steps
- ⌜⌟ Removable panal on Plaza deck
- o□o Manhole covers

Service entrances to Plaza stores and residential entrances to top floors are located on side streets.

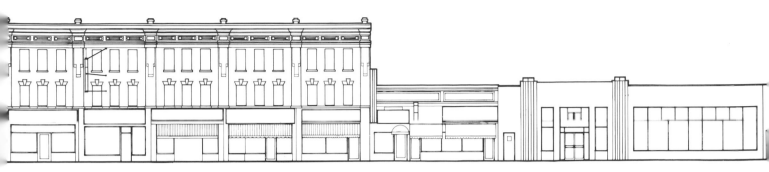

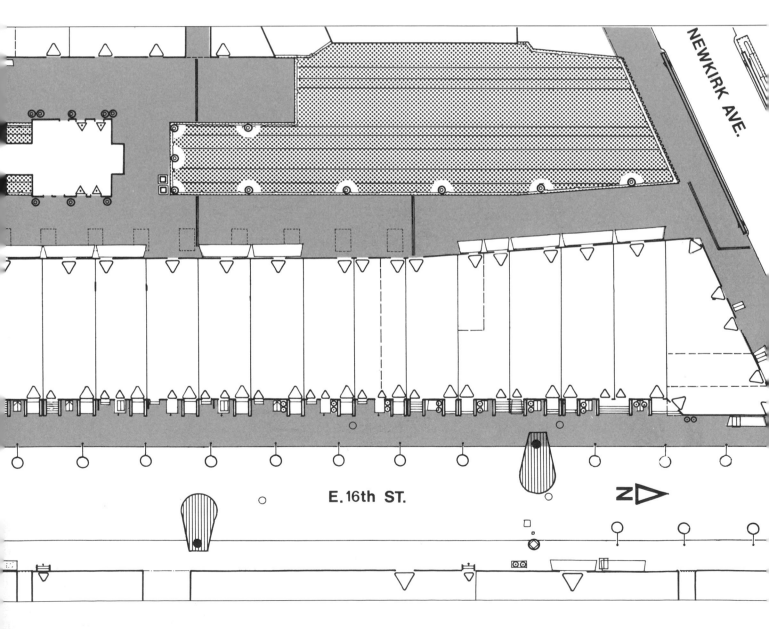

E. 16th ST.

NEWKIRK AVE.

Metal shields and bridge girders obstruct visibility.

Street lacks unity; station house is run down.

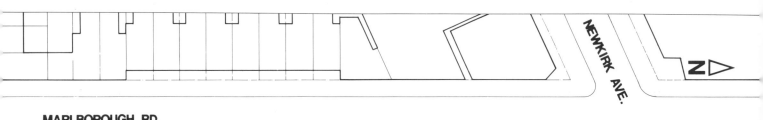

NEWKIRK AVE.

N

MARLBOROUGH RD.

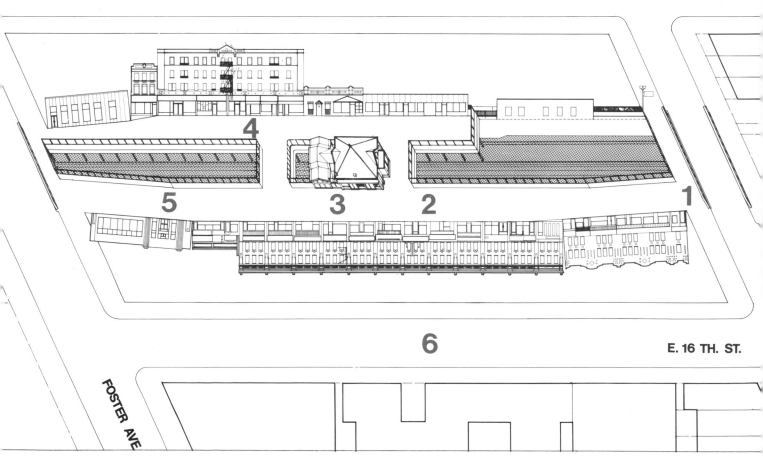

4

5   3   2   1

6   E. 16 TH. ST.

FOSTER AVE.

The deck is barren without amenities.

Unattractive fence and lights surround the parapet wall.

Critical issues uncovered

Everyone was beginning to see in detail the problems that had to be overcome.

1 The first problem was inadequate visibility. Though Newkirk was easily accessible, bridge girders and high corrugated metal shields made it difficult for pedestrians and drivers to actually *see* the plaza or sense its presence.

2 The second problem was that the plaza had no particular image. Its unique deck above the subway station gave a certain definition and identity to the space, but nothing had been done over the years to emphasize or embellish this space as an urban phenomenon. There was a serious lack of uniformity; each business had its own storefront design, its own sign, and in all but a few cases, its own awnings. A few merchants regularly displayed their goods outside, but the majority did not. There was no directory listing the plaza's range of retail and service activities. This lack of a design theme was recognized, and became a key in the design approach to the improvement of the plaza.

3 The third problem was that the station house needed work. Right in the center of the plaza, a functional as well as visual focus, it clearly needed renovation to make it an attractive building and a more pleasant component of the total scheme.

4 The fourth problem pertained to the deck of the plaza. Structural deterioration had eroded a great deal of the deck's surface. The vistas of cracked gray concrete were barren and drab, hardly a pleasant setting for attracting shoppers.

5 Finally, there was the lack of amenities. Landscaping, game tables, benches—items that would have made the plaza more inviting—were absent. The lighting along the chain-link parapets, overlooking the station, was of very low intensity and ugly; in the evening, this situation discouraged people from using the space, thus limiting the sales volume of its shops and restaurants. None of this was helped by the fact that physical maintenance was below standard, perhaps as a result of shared jurisdiction over the plaza by the New York City Transit Authority and the city; each expecting the other would take the responsibility of maintenance tasks.

6 In addition, there were certain detracting aspects of the immediate neighborhood. The side streets, mainly residential, were used either for servicing the plaza shops or as access to the apartments above. These streets were inadequately maintained and cleaned. Parking regulations weren't enforced. Entrances and building facades needed refurbishing. Clearly the character and condition of these streets had an adverse impact on the general ambience of the area.

The community considered horizontal banners as a design option. It was rejected because of maintenance problems.

The design proposal

By this time, following close consultation with the community, the Urban Design Group began to work on alternative design concepts for consideration. Two things had been defined: the character of Newkirk Plaza, and the problems standing in the way of strengthening its character.

Newkirk's special charm was not derived from its architecturally significant buildings. It was unique because of the commodious but run down deck that created a spacial separation of pedestrians from both the subway and cars. The designers sought to emphasize the difference in levels through a design that would unify plaza activities on all levels, making the transition more appealing for the pedestrian. The emphasis was on instilling and sustaining a festive atmosphere through eye-catching, people-oriented events such as street closings and the provision of seating, plantings, awnings, and coordinated signs.

With this in mind, three major design alternatives were presented, including a variety of options for individual fixtures. Many colorful but simple drawings helped the community visualize the three choices.

The first alternative consisted of colorful banners, stretched tent-style over the plaza, connecting the facades of the bordering buildings with the parapet walls that overlook the subway. Suspending horizontal banners across this space emphasized, instead of playing down, the fact that there were trains and people moving in and out down below.

The second alternative consisted of an overhead structure, a lightweight composition of acrylic panels, to provide year-round protection from inclement weather. This plan also included continuous awnings, tying the various storefronts together visually to make them appear more of a unit. Such awnings could be either fixed or roll-up, and could be made of vinyl, canvas, or plexiglass.

The third alternative consisted of only covering the seating areas, giving shelter to pedestrians, and providing a colorful canopy running along the outer edge of the shops.

Then there were discussions on overall improvements; each included an analysis of mainte-

A metal frame canopy over the plaza was another design alternative. This was rejected by the community because of high construction costs.

The community was receptive to this modest design alternative. However, the canopy structure on the right was dropped from the final plan.

nance, durability and price.

Various treatments for the paving of the plaza deck were illustrated: colored cement, brick pavers, tiles, or just painting. The chain-link fence surrounding the subway cut might be repainted, it was suggested, using it as a trellis for newly planted runs of ivy. Or it might be replaced by a fence of decorative wrought iron. The wrought iron fence, which was the preferred alternative, turned out to be much too expensive, however. A variety of planters — wood ones, concrete ones, plastic ones — with different species of trees and bushes were proposed. As for seating, various sizes and makes of benches and tables were presented. Lighting alternatives included a range of locations, installations, and stylistic types, from fixtures of an antique ''early New York'' character to more modern ones.

The community had the option of cleaning,

painting or restoring building facades, depending on the building material. The parapet wall, the blank walls of the building facades, the girders running above the roadway, and the passageway leading into the plaza precinct from Marlborough Road were to be painted.

Better signs on storefronts and an information kiosk at the plaza entrance were proposed to enhance the visibility of the plaza. All-weather works of art, such as sculpture and murals, would cover blank walls. A detailed list of the needed improvements for the structure of the subway and of its stationhouse was reconsidered. The community evaluated the different alternatives on the basis of economic and esthetic ramifications. Every detail was scrutinized in terms of desirability and cost.

The idea of banners was dropped because of the high cost of maintenance. The art department of the Off-Track Betting Corporation had supplied the concepts for the banners, which was exciting, but in the final analysis, the community could not justify the money involved.

The concept of an overall enclosure for the plaza was also rejected. In addition to being concerned about the cost, people thought it was important to preserve the open character of the plaza and be able to see the sky. The option of roofing the seating areas was also not accepted, not only because of the expense, but also because an extended roof would create an elongated, vertical passageway to the station house, rather than accentuating the seating and recreational areas of the plaza.

As one might expect, the final proposal included a combination of ideas from various alternatives. It maintained the plaza as an open air environment. The awnings, meant to unify the plaza's storefronts, were accepted enthusiastically. So was the partial brick paving of the plaza's deck, including the entrance areas at the end of the plaza and the decorative edge along the parapet walls.

Budget was a constant decisive factor. The community opted for a good looking and affordable solution.

Refining the design concept

Now that a clear idea had emerged of what the community wanted, the final design scheme phase began. The designers went through street furniture catalogs and samples of materials and fixtures. Contractors and suppliers were contacted to provide more information about the physical feasibility and detailed cost estimates of the various options.

In meeting after meeting with the task force, every item was considered in light of similar standards. Would the proposed item enhance the intrinsic character of Newkirk and fit the total design concept? Were its initial cost, the cost of its installation, and the cost of its maintenance within the community's means? Would it be feasible to integrate the specific idea into the phased implementation of the project? Would it be durable and safe? And would its location impede access in the event of emergencies? The options were

thus narrowed down, and the proposal refined accordingly.

Meanwhile, the Flatbush Development Corporation and the Community Planning Board organized follow-up meetings to discuss securing financial support from various interest groups, the Off-Track Betting Corporation, the banks on the plaza, Brooklyn Union Gas Company, New York Telephone, and Consolidated Edison.

The Urban Design Group identified the various city agencies with jurisdiction over the plaza. The Department of Highways was responsible for the bridges over the subway cut; the Traffic Department was in charge of parking; the Bureau of Gas and Electricity was in control of the utilities, including the streetlights. Finally, there was the Transit Authority, overseeing the deck of the plaza and its lighting.

The local newspapers kept the public informed about day-to-day progress, something very crucial to any street-saving initiative in terms of community confidence and eventual financial contributions.

The second phase — developing the plan, refining the preliminary scheme — took about six weeks. After all, Newkirk was not embarking on a futuristic solution for the year 2000; people wanted something the community could enjoy within one to two years, if not sooner.

The emergence of a plan

It was a practical, lasting, little renaissance that was finally to emerge from all the community participation and design input. The phased plan stressed feasibility in terms of cost and allowed for immediate implementation. The final proposal also illustrated how the initial solutions could lead to long-term improvements in the area. Newkirk's modest plan maintained its uniqueness and grass roots quality. This is evident in the highlights of the final design proposal.

Stationary canvas awnings would be mounted below the signs of the stores, and along both the eastern and western edges of the plaza. The two colors on the awnings were repeated in other improvements. Across from each store, an identifying sign would be placed on the parapet wall.

The first financial support came from these proud merchants who participated in the project throughout the revitalization.

The facades of the buildings would be steam-cleaned and repaired. Cornices would be restored and painted. The parapet walls and fences would be sandblasted, as would the station house, thus restoring the quality of its original facade. Sculpture would be placed in appropriate locations. Blank walls would be brightened with murals. Improved graphics on signs and information boards would be designed to facilitate directions.

The plaza's deck would be structurally repaired, and the proposed seating areas would be delineated by decorative paving titles. Green outdoor carpet would be installed in front of the

stores to articulate outdoor selling space under the awnings.

To heighten the plaza's visibility and allure, new signs and street lighting would be mounted at its two entrances, and at the Marlborough Road passageway. In addition, the power of existing lighting would be increased, and the old fixtures would be replaced by more decorative heads. The Brooklyn Union Gas Company contributed new gas lamps on the sidewalks at the plaza's entrances.

The bridge girders would be painted with a vivid graphic design, thus lending some color to the view first seen as one approaches the area.

The corrugated metal fences at the ends of the subway cut would be covered by painted, graffiti-proof, aluminum panels.

New signs would be installed above the subway tracks, changing the name of the station from Newkirk Avenue to, naturally, Newkirk Plaza. Directories of the plaza's shops and services would be installed at the plaza's entrances and on the subway platform, reminding people that this is more than a train stop, it is a place for shopping, fun, and relaxation.

Seating areas would be located along the parapet walls and concentrated near the entrances. Wooden benches with backs, game tables, planters, and litter baskets would be placed in these locations. Bicycle racks would also be provided at the entrances.

Outdoor cafes would be established by several of the plaza's restaurants, in places convenient both to their owners and to the general flow of pedestrians.

A full-time porter would be hired by the Merchants Association to be responsible for maintenance and repairs. Lighting fixtures along the parapet walls would continue to be maintained by the Transit Authority. The task force would remain the pivotal and organizing force, providing a list of distributors and contractors for the replacement of parts and the servicing of the various improvements. The task force would also work with the owners on East 16th Street and on Marlborough Road toward upgrading their properties; painting doorways and window frames, and help distinguish between commercial delivery entrances and residential ones.

The final plan strongly recommended that parking regulations be enforced on the surrounding streets to allow for a better flow of traffic on Newkirk Avenue, and to facilitate regular street sweeping. Parking meters that didn't work would be replaced.

All of these recommendations were carefully considered since they were a result of a continuous process that involved the participation of the residents, the merchants, and the pertinent city agencies. That is why, at Newkirk, participatory planning rather than confrontation, became the force behind immediate visible change.

Plaza before the improvement.
Right: With modest means a new image will emerge. The improved Plaza will attract more shoppers and encourage people to sit, stroll and enjoy themselves.

MARLBOROUGH RD.

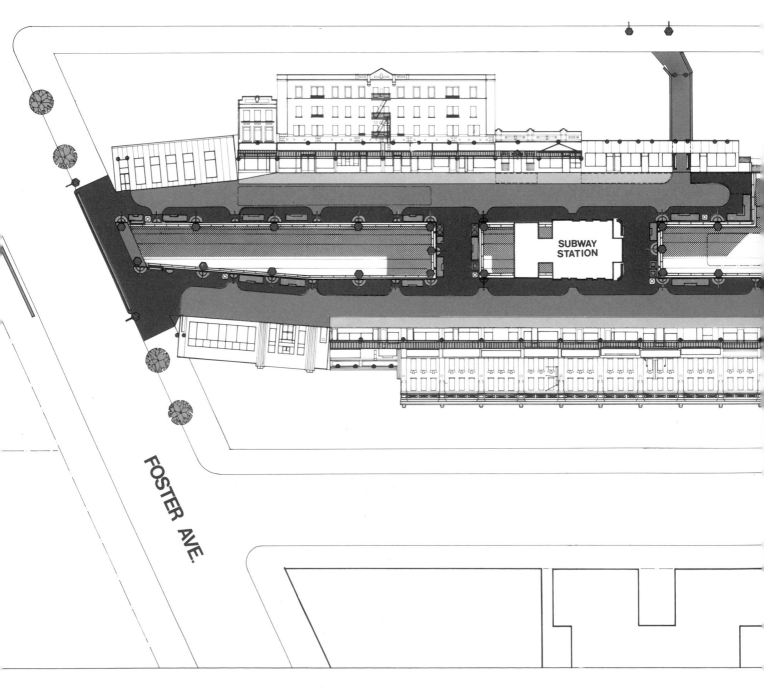

FOSTER AVE.

SUBWAY STATION

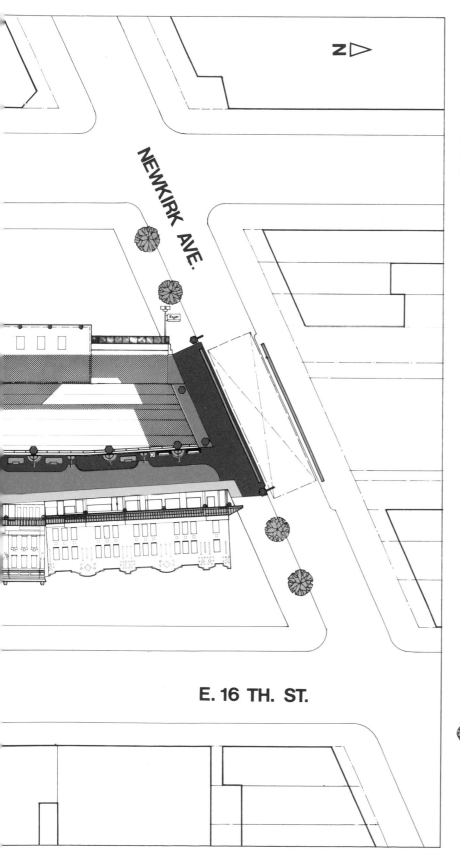

NEWKIRK AVE.

N ▷

E. 16 TH. ST.

The proposed plan:

In the upgraded Newkirk Plaza, the deck and subway station house will be renovated. The awnings and the decorative paving defining seating areas will strengthen Newkirk Plaza as a magnet for residents and visitors. Well designed lighting fixtures on the sidewalk and painted girders at the entrances, will signal drivers that this place is special.

Legend:

Plaza surface treatment
Surface and storefronts
Outdoor eating area
Benches and tables
Planters
Trash bins
Painting on fence
Billboard on fence
New Light fixture
New light on building
New sidewalk lighting
New trees
New awning
Store signs
Directory & Exhibit
Facade treatment
Bicycle racks
Concrete ledge
Area for art work
No parking any time

Above: Decorated lights and painted girders at Plaza's entrance.

Upper left: Detail of Plaza deck before improvement.
Left: Plaza deck after improvement.

Below: Upgraded passageway to Marlborough Road is painted and lit.

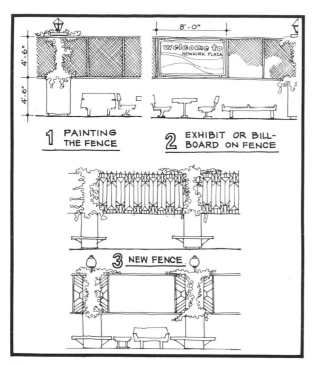

Above: Detail of new fences and benches attached to parapet wall.

Above: The design of a street furniture unit combining seating, planting, lighting and signs.

Below: Detailed dimensions and materials for benches and fence.

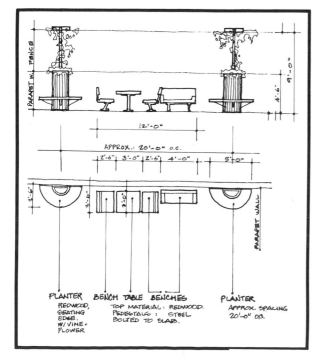

Below: Alternative light fixtures for the Plaza related to pedestrian scale

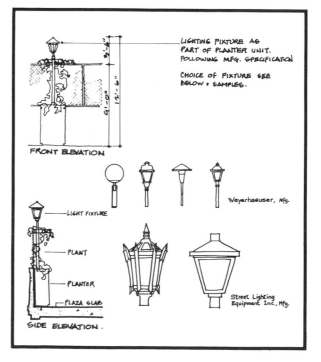

Implementing the plan

The process of translating concepts into action and implementation has to be planned as thoroughly as any physical improvement. While the design process may appear more exciting and creative, in the presentation of colorful drawings, its success is dependent on the organization and management of its implementation. Newkirk Plaza action plan will give you the detailed procedure and tasks encountered in this phase.

At Newkirk, the action plan was broken down into three tasks. The first task was to prepare a draft of the budget and to identify sources of funding. The second was the preparation of schedules of construction. The third task was to develop a program of maintenance to ensure upkeep and management. The task force was to coordinate the plan from start to finish.

Budget drafts were prepared at the time that the first design concepts were formulated. Community approval had been based, from the earliest stage, not only on design analysis but on realistic evaluation of different options, based on durability and cost of materials.

Alternative itemized budgets had been prepared for Newkirk. They ranged from major high-cost, long range improvements, such as paving the entire deck with handsome brick, to less costly, short-range improvements, such as covering the deck with a decorative waterproof paint.

While the budget draft concentrated on costs, the first phase of implementation focused also on resources to pay for the plan. The design options and their exact funding needs were useful as funding resources were sought. A precise cost estimate presented with the drawings and diagrams, made the difference in the attitude of potential contributors. It gave them a confidence in the professionalism of the planners and reassured them about the serious nature of the project.

Several public and private sources had been identified. Much of the money was in the form of government grants. It was agreed that each grant would be managed separately, according to the requirements of its source. Eventually, specific grants were assigned to cover the cost of different elements of the plan. This enabled each agency to monitor its funding directly.

Three groups were appointed by the Newkirk Task Force to receive and allocate funds for the project. Two were community organizations: The Flashbush Development Corporation and the Newkirk Plaza Merchants Association; the third was a municipal agency, the New York City Transit Authority. Together, they formed a funding committee to manage and raise money.

Securing financial help

The Flatbush Development Corporation and the Transit Authority together raised $752,000. Of this total sum, $400,000 was given by the federal government through UMPTA for the rehabilitation of the deck structure; another $300,000 from the state and city covered rehabilitation expenses for the plaza, including the provision of the various amenities. Furthermore, the merchants group collected $52,000 from their own members.

This $52,000, raised by thirty-four merchants may seem like a small amount, but it was the first funding the project received and had a major symbolic impact. It demonstrated local dedication and led other prospective sources to follow. It was agreed that this money would go toward improving the private property lining the plaza: steam cleaning, facade painting, lighting for the buildings, and the provision of individual awnings. Off-Track Betting contributed a mechanical sweeper to help keep the plaza clean. Some of the money was also used for paying a private porter to keep the plaza maintained. The New York Telephone Company called up to say they would contribute decorative phone booths. Con Edison agreed to pay for the hook-up of new electrical lamps, rather than the quaint gas ones initially hoped for by the community. The merchants agreed to pay for the bills and maintenance. These incentives were the base for the funding committee to launch a public-sector campaign to cover the more major, costly improvements.

Federal funds

The Transit Authority set out to identify and receive federal grants for the largest jobs in the project. There were two reasons for their involvement. First, the plaza is over a major subway station which is under the jurisdiction of the Transit Authority. This gave the Authority considerable bargaining power with the Federal Urban Mass Transportation Authority for the allocation of special transit funds to use on Newkirk improvements. This agency pursued the special transit funds for the improvements of the subway structure and stationhouse.

Secondly, the Transit Authority was the only public agency involved that could actually arrange for, manage, and get construction contracts, and this operational capacity provided a dependable bridge between concept and implementation. The federal government prefers giving grants to the local agency that is technically the funding recipient since it can manage physical improvements and enter into contractual relationships.

The Transit Authority also requested a $400,000 capital grant from the Federal Aid to Urban Systems program (FAUS). FAUS funds would go toward upgrading the structure of the plaza, especially its deck's deteriorated underpinnings. While FAUS supplied the major share, the city was required to put up twenty per cent of the total amount. The city's share was later guaranteed in the New York City Capital Budget.

The Transit Authority was also assigned to receive and manage funds from the Community Development program, which is backed by the federal government and coordinated by the U.S. Department of Housing and Urban Development (HUD). These funds are available for neighborhoods around the city. Obtaining a share of these funds for Newkirk was expedited by the Flatbush Development Corporation, through political pressure. Both the City Planning Commission and the Brooklyn Borough President were requested by the Flatbush Development Corporation to give Newkirk high priority amid the many disparate requests for allocations in this highly competitive funding category. As a result, the Authority received $150,000 from this program.

Every funding program has different rules; the allocation and management of a program's funds must reflect them. For example, the rules of the Community Development program stipulated that those funds could not go directly to the task force, that they had to go to a city operating agency — in this case, the Transit Authority —

with the legal mandate to spend those funds and let out construction contracts. Furthermore, C.D. funding could only be used for the cost of improvements, themselves. Therefore, these funds paid for the decorative paving, the rewiring of new lampheads, the treatment and upgrading of the subway control house, and its fences and parapet walls.

State funds

The Brooklyn Borough President did not just approach city hall on the behalf of Newkirk, he also went to Albany, the state capital, where, with the aid of two local assemblymen and a state senator, he successfully lobbied for a budget appropriation of $150,000 from the State Supplemental Budget, an appropriation made for community revitalization. The Flatbush Development Corporation managed this sum, and in contrast to the Community Development funds, those monies from the state allow more flexibility. They can cover design, management, and labor costs. In the case of Newkirk, this $150,000 paid for painting the bridge girders, installing the gas lamps, and for putting in benches, planters, tables, and murals. Some of it also went to pay a project director who was responsible to develop a work program and schedule all improvement, and for a graphic design consultant. Neither Community Development or state funds allow their money to pay for private improvements. It was therefore the money raised by merchants that was used to improve private properties.

The construction begins

Newkirk Plaza improvement is well underway. The building facades have been steam cleaned, the Transit Authority, acting as the architect and engineer of the deck, completed the specification drawings. All the construction has been scheduled to minimize interference with the day to day life of the plaza. A good deal of the work is done in the hours of least activity on the plaza.

The task force retained the power to review any problems that arise. For example, should a style or make of a lamp initially decided on be discontinued, or be out of stock, representatives

Facades of buildings after cleaning.

of the task force can expedite another make, place the order, and maintain the overall schedule. As changes are called for, or if the schedule is adjusted, the task force meets and the Newkirk community as a whole is thus informed on both the progress and problems of their project as it moves ahead.

Continued community involvement

A plan for maintenance was the crucial, consolidating step in the implementation process. For only through planned maintenance can the plaza's revitalization be meaningful for the lasting enjoyment of the community.

The Newkirk Plaza Merchants Association has assumed the ongoing, long term task of maintaining the plaza. They have agreed to pay for any additional maintenance help that may be needed, and to share the expenses of removing litter. They have also pledged to take care of the plants,

to look after the furnishings on the plaza, and to continue to keep up their own establishments. The task force is routinely supplying the merchants with up-to-date lists of distributors, retailers, and, contractors so that replacement and repair of the various amenities can be expedited. The merchants' commitment is an example of community self-reliance at a basic level.

The Transit Authority technically presides over the entire plaza and its platform levels, but the daily maintenance of the deck level itself will be in the hands of the merchants. The Highway Department will have jurisdiction over the streets, of course, and over the bridge girders. Parking will continue to be supervised by the Traffic Department; trash collection will go on being handled by the City's Sanitation Department. The staff of the New York City Planning Department, in consultation with the Urban Design Group, will coordinate the participation of all municipal public agencies.

The Flatbush Development Corporation, as an active agency reflecting community opinion, will report to the task force. And in turn, the task force will, with the help of municipal agencies, community groups, business groups, utility companies, and private interests, seek to solve all problems in the best interest of the Newkirk community.

The revitalization of Newkirk Plaza seems a small improvement when compared to some of the large, extensive, showcase projects across the country. Yet, no project and no community is too small to be improved. It is the process of working with a community, step by step, from inception to conclusion, that is as important as the end product itself. The Urban Design Group did not want to wipe clean the slate of the street's character, and start from scratch. It sought to embellish the mosaic of physical and human energy that had already been there for many years.

Although the scale of the revitalization at Newkirk was small, the task was not easy, to be sure. The initial design process took almost two years; funding took about eighteen months, from the time the grants were applied for until the time they were in hand. Construction will take another six to eight months, and maintenance, the final community involvement, will never end, we hope.

In Newkirk, the process and actions of revitalizations have inspired the community to care about the plaza as if it were an extension of their own living rooms. The principles and procedures used here, and their results, can engender such enthusiasm in many communities. What is happening at Newkirk is a transferable triumph.

Labors of love like that just traced at Newkirk Plaza are increasingly apparent in many neighborhoods around the country. Concerned citizens are orchestrating a comeback for their urban cores. Newkirk is a resonant reminder that even subway stops can be named desire.

Lighting is installed.

REVITALIZING BEACH 20th STREET

Far Rockaway, in the Queens section of New York City, is a peninsula. In the early years of this century, its popularity as a resort was spurred by a railroad linking it with five nearby towns. And because of the area's well-integrated transit systems, Beach 20th Street, a lively retail and commercial stretch, became Far Rockaway's main line of service, shopping, and sauntering, not only for those visiting the shore in summers, but also for the quiet, year-round residential neighborhood surrounding it.

By the 1940's Far Rockaway had reached its peak as a leisure and recreational spot for working-class families. The ensuing decline was brought on by changing economic patterns and changing transportation patterns. The popularity of the private car supplanted the romance and rapidity of the trains. New shopping centers in the region diverted the devotions and dollars of people. The retail sections of Beach 20th got bypassed; once thriving, they were thwarted by competition. New bridges made car trips from Far Rockaway to the mainland even easier. So the once-crowded beaches became only a local attraction, their area-wide allure diminished by the car. Also, an expanded highway network made possible a summertime exodus to competing hinterlands and beachheads farther and farther removed.

While Beach 20th remained a retail street, and maintained its small-town, year-round commercial atmosphere, some businesses began to pull out. Plastic, metal or fake brick was put on many of the buildings, perhaps with an eye to making them seem more flashy and modern. In this sense, during the 1940's and 1950's, the condi-

Left: Street before improvements showing traffic and pedestrian congestion.
Map below: Location of Beach 20th Street and its mass transit links

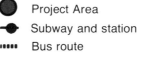

● Project Area
Subway and station
ııııı Bus route

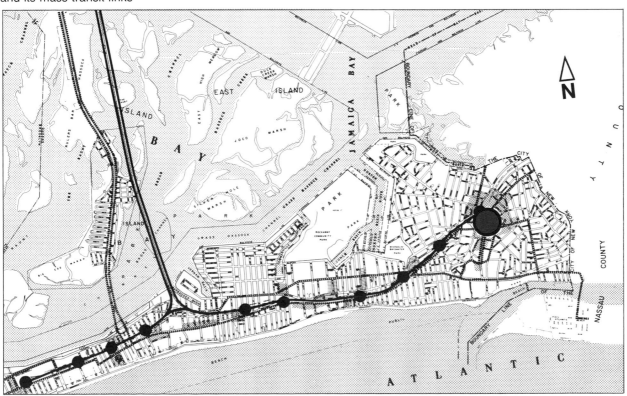

tion of Beach 20th typified many American shopping streets lingering on from an era when close-knit communities, like those of the Far Rockaway peninsula, made up much of "urban" America.

The activities along the street ranged from clothing stores, to churches and synagogues, to an appetizing assortment of mom-and-pop stores, to hardware stores, banks, and markets. The shopkeepers knew the shoppers; many of the businesses had been there for two or three generations, comprising a stabilizing force. Even with all the changes in the physical condition of the street, the shoppers continued to come. The street's scale remained intact, with apartments above retail, where people can look out their windows and see what's going on. It was still a familiar street, with community feeling unlike a big shopping center.

While these qualities helped to maintain interest of people in their street, it was a major concern for everyone that people were increasingly being turned off by noise and the declining image of the street.

Beach 20th had become loud and rundown. Cars made it difficult for people to tarry, exchange pleasantries, and simply take their time. The street had also become a delivery zone for trucks. Parking for the cars was insufficient. The sidewalks were too narrow. Utility poles, parking signs, traffic signals and signs, parking meters, a few trees—all had been put in place, over the years, without any coordination. Street lighting was insufficient too, and benches, where they appeared at all, were ugly and uncomfortable.

This dismal state of affairs on one hand, and the political constituency representing residents and businesses of Beach 20th Street on the other, caused the immediate sense of urgency which generated a plan.

The initial plan

In the early 1970's, the Borough Office of the City Planning Department in Queens, having daily contact with the community, commissioned a planning study to identify the major problems in the area that needed action. This report, released in 1973, emphasized three specific improvements: basic highway improvements and repairs; mod-

ifying the width of the roads around Beach 20th to facilitate the movement of traffic; and creating more parking.

A task force was also formed then, the Far Rockaway Revitalization Task Force, which included a number of merchants, residents, representatives of the Borough Office, the mayor's office, and other city agencies. It was this group that would draw up subsequent plans based on the 1973 recommendations, and soon they generated new studies of the marketing and transportation patterns. The Borough Office pitched in, and by 1974, everyone involved had a good grasp of the main issues and problems.

Based on these studies, a grant was secured from the Federal Community Development Program. A sum of $1.3 million was earmarked strictly for the road work and parking provisions recommended in the report. While that report had emphasized getting people into the area by car, and allowing them to find a parking spot, it had not addressed the improvement of the street's environment for the shoppers. It is one thing to get people into an area; it is quite another to *keep* them there. While recognizing the need for more parking, the task force sensed that something vital was being left out.

A new street image as part of the plan

A man named Sidney Baumgarten, then an assistant to the mayor, realized that something essential was missing: a street is more than just a road.

He suggested to the Far Rockaway Revitalization Committee that a much more total approach would be needed if the overall image of Beach 20th was to be improved. He also proposed that the physical image of the street was basic to securing the economic objectives and was as important as wider roads and more parking.

It was then that the committee requested that the Urban Design Group become involved. The first thing that struck the designers, much as it had Baumgarten, was that the $1.3 million wouldn't guarantee that people would come to Beach 20th. While the inadequate parking was a main reason for the street's chaotic state, and while most of the residents thought of revitaliza-

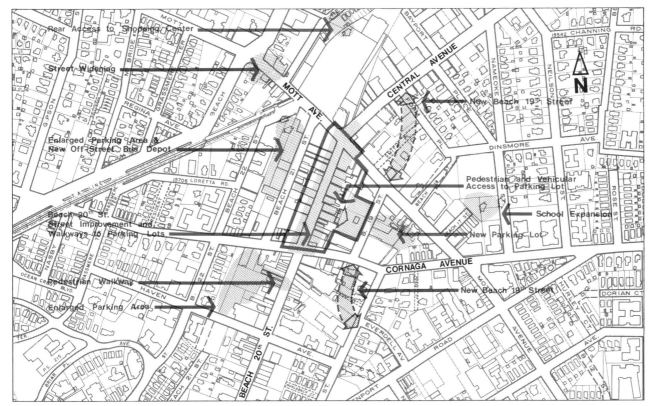

Original improvements around Beach
20th Street, included in the
Community Development Program,
were mostly traffic and parking oriented.

tion as a fancy term for more parking, a healthy, lively street must also be convenient for those who get there on foot. And it must be an agreeable place for people to walk from store to store. It was clear that bringing Beach 20 back as *the* attraction meant suggesting improvements that would enliven the pedestrian experience.

Meeting the challenge of pedestrian comfort did not mean that the projected parking improvement took a back seat. The main point is that a balance was sought: the provision of ample parking coupled with the provision of an affable pedestrian environment. But a crucial question remained. How was this more comprehensive approach going to work when the available money was budgeted only for road widening and parking lots? This meant looking again at the assumptions behind that initial allocation of $1.3 million.

That money had been earmarked for area-wide improvements, specifically the widening of the roads around Beach 20th, the construction of a new parking lot for 108 cars on Beach 19th, enlarging an existing parking lot on Beach 21st and providing a bus-loading zone. The designers found that out of that $1.3 million, $300,000 had been targeted for road work along Beach 20th itself. They suggested that these funds if rechanneled, would be enough to make pedestrian and environmental improvements *without* threatening the projected parking.

To convince the Revitalization Committee to go in this direction the designers also had to convince the government sponsors of the grant that it made sense to redirect some money toward the improvements of the street's environment. The merchants had to see several drawings showing what Beach 20th would be like after improvements, and how the business climate would be improved. The government sponsors looking after the grant were similarly given a more vivid idea of the pragmatic as well as creative possibilities. The fact that the government went along was a major victory in the Beach 20th Street story. And indeed, the Community Development Program in general has become more flexible. No longer are grants targeted toward street improvements restricted solely to roadwork and parking, because many cases around the country have demonstrated that establishing an atmosphere of convenience, and visual attractiveness along a street is a basic element of neighborhood revitalization.

Certainly, in the case of Beach 20th, the designers' approach was a key factor in changing the target of the $300,000 allocation. Once everyone saw the possibilities in strong visual terms, it was easier to accept the change. Encouraged, local branch banks loaned seed money and began considering matching grants. Several businesses also pledged money. These additional funds were directed toward restoring and painting individual stores, toward the overall maintenance of the streets, and toward the purchase of new street furniture.

Issues emerge and goals are defined

The primary goal of the revitalization effort was to bring back an attractive image that could in turn bring back Beach 20th's vigor by giving people a real alternative to the impersonality and plasticity of the big shopping centers.

This economic issue guided the designers' strategy. By building upon the community awareness and participation that were already in place, and by citing the economic benefits of making the street more attractive, they were also demonstrating how retail strips could be brightened, thus generating more confidence and investment. They were also concerned with ensuring a safe setting for shoppers, many of whom come to Beach 20th in the late afternoon or evenings.

As the study began, specific problems emerged. Collecting and analyzing data enabled the designers and community to understand prob-

lems in detail, and sometimes confirmed issues that had seemed obvious to everyone. For example, the specific patterns of traffic were recorded —where it moved, from what directions, and in what relative volumes at different points along the street. The street's hardware was studied and a scoring system was set up for noting the physical condition of the street itself, its sidewalks, and the buildings adjoining them.

The process of collecting information did not scrutinize the entire Far Rockaway area in much detail, or even all of Beach 20th. Instead, general information was gathered on the larger impact area, while the detailed work was concentrated on the block of Beach 20th running between Mott and Cornaga avenues, the neighborhood's basic retail core.

Identifying the conflicts

By analyzing the impact area and the details of that one block, the designers were able to better understand the physical forces acting upon Beach 20th, as well as the influence the residential makeup of the surrounding area had on the economic and social characteristics of the street. They were also able to understand how the dynamics of such forces, acting over the years, had negatively affected the street's condition and climate. Giving the data graphic representation — as in Little Italy and Newkirk Plaza, with maps, elevations, and sections — allowed the task force direct, practical visualization of the street's problems.

Three critical issues became apparent:
● There was considerable congestion along Beach 20th. It had become a chaotic thoroughfare connecting the five towns out in Nassau County, on Long Island's nearby south shore, with the beach. This traffic disrupted the street's ongoing function as a retail core. Moreover, with parallel parking for cars, and with a lot of double-parked delivery trucks, pedestrians on both sides of the street found themselves dodging traffic. Often, when they tried pulling their own cars away from the curb, the double-parked trucks were in the way.
● The sidewalks were much too narrow. Pedestrian crossings were dangerous. And there was crowding at the bus stops. These conflicts, aggra-

cade Deterioration   Vacant Stores   Visual&Physical Obstruction by Trees & Vehicles   Congestion at Bus Stop   Dangerous Crossin

BEACH 20th ST.

MOTT AVE.

adequate Street Lighting   Overhead Poles   Stores without Underground Elec. Service   Pedestrian Congestion   Vehicular Congestion

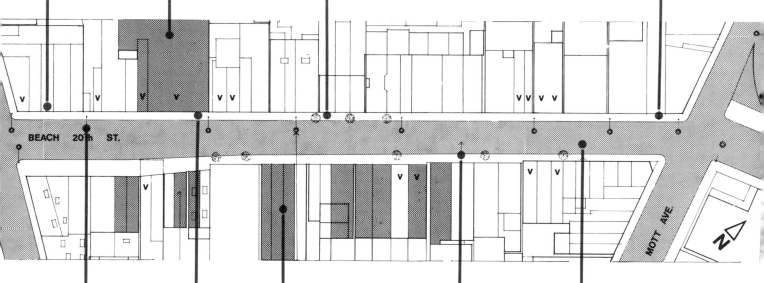

vated by the vehicular congestion, resulted in frequent jaywalking in and out between the parked cars and trucks.

● In addition to the conflict between cars and people, visual clutter and physical deterioration were grievous. Most important visually were the huge, high utility poles, with overhead wires running between them. Looking down Beach 20th, they dominated the view. And, on closer observation the signs on many of the buildings were garish and dilapidated. The facades of the buildings had either been modernized with cheap finishes or left to decay. The bed of the street itself was a mess of cracks. Such hardware as meters, traffic signs, and benches were scattered.

In pointing out these critical issues, the designers were more than supported by the public's response to a questionnaire they had sent around the community. People identified these same issues as the most important for the future of the street.

No room for the pedestrian

There were several reasons for all this congestion. The street was both a thoroughfare and a retail core. The forty two metered parking places, were being used most of the time and forced the double-parking of trucks; also, the owners of the various businesses had long-term parking times on many meters, whereas the shoppers, having pulled up to the curb and parked, had short-term times. The owners' convenience limited the shoppers' options to park along the street. With all the cars dodging each other, there was frequently only one lane open for moving traffic.

The traffic loads at peak hours were heavy. On weekdays, for instance, at noon, the load reached 500 vehicles per hour in one direction. And the count on nearby streets dramatized even further the impact on Beach 20th. At its intersection with Mott, for example, the count was 700! This daily explosion of traffic all around this particular block, added noise and pollution, constituting a crippling atmosphere for the strolling shopper.

The pedestrian environment was appalling. The sidewalks were too narrow, so pedestrians spilled out into the street, looking over their shoulders to make sure they weren't going to get hit. People getting off the subway at the Mott Avenue station

were bumping into each other. Those exiting the buses at Mott and Beach 20th, heading toward the shops had to cross Mott in the face of turning traffic; jaywalking added to the confusion. The pedestrian felt uncomfortable or, worse, threatened.

The planners measured pedestrian comfort by observations in the field, confirmed with research. The rule of thumb is there has to be at least two and a half feet of sidewalk width per person for two people to pass each other without interference. For busy shopping streets like Beach 20th, it was concluded that at least three people should be able to walk side by side comfortably. Taking into account the fact that shoppers must also have some space — given that many are laden with parcels, or open umbrellas on rainy days — it was established that the *minimum clear path* along each sidewalk should be two and a half feet times three, or almost eight feet. Beach 20th couldn't provide this recommended minimum. Its regular sidewalk width at the time was seven and a half feet. In places it was nine. But there were all the meters, mailboxes, and utility poles getting in the way of achieving an adequately clear sidewalk area.

The Urban Design Group proposed widening the sidewalks. The new widths would be from twelve to fifteen feet, thus eliminating the metered parking places and creating a newly aligned vehicular right-of-way varying in width from twenty six to thirty feet (the wider measure for bus stops). The original alignment for the *total* street had varied in width from fifty to sixty feet. Two lanes for moving traffic, a standing lane on alternate sides of the street for the use of delivery trucks, and the much-needed widening of the sidewalks were created. This proposal related both traffic needs and pedestrian movement.

The idea of eliminating curbside parking was the most controversial among the members of the task force. Two camps emerged. The first camp consisted of the resident shoppers. They perceived that less parking right on the street would make walking more desirable, thus increasing the number of shoppers. But even the more mild mannered in this camp asked, "Couldn't at least *one* side of the street be retained for parking?" The second camp included the merchants and

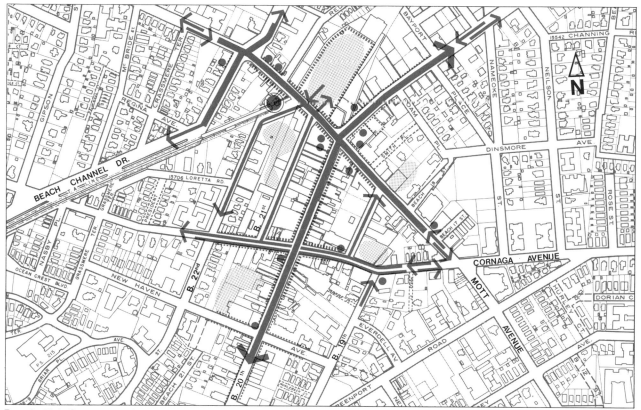

Beach 20th Street remains a main throughfare for vehicles to the beach. Existing circulation map demonstrates comparatively heavy traffic.

other property owners, who felt that less available parking would reduce the number of shoppers. Others frankly resented the thought of losing the parking space in front of their own shops, since they had gotten used to parking their *own* cars there. "Give us more parking, not less," they shouted.

This fear of losing customers has been the main objective voiced by merchants everywhere when the reduction of number of cars or relocation of parking has been proposed. The attachment between commerce and the car has become such an engrained element of American thinking that, until quite recently, merchants have automatically shied away from pedestrian-oriented plans.

By way of responding to the resistance on Beach 20th, the designers proposed an alternative:

constructing a 108-place parking lot over one block, off Beach 19th, directly to the rear of Beach 20th stores. This would replace the forty two spaces along the street. The designers also proposed a direct access to the parking lot from the Beach 20th side. This pedestrianway would be tree-lined with attractive paving and murals on the blank side walls. The plan strengthened the provision that the merchants felt was vital — "more parking, not less" — at the same time making the case for freeing the sidewalks for pedestrian enjoyment.

While car access to a street, or ample parking within an enjoyable walk of it, is surely essential, there are increasing numbers of cases where the emphasis on planning for the pedestrian has been a key to economic success. National surveys confirm that streetfront parking does not

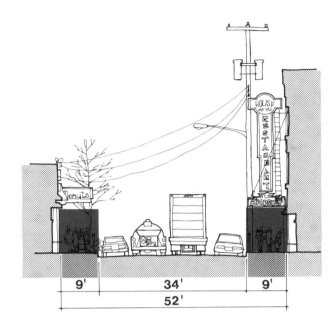

Existing section at the middle of the block. Parking lanes on both sides of the street occupy nearly half of the street bed, leave only two lanes for moving traffic.

Proposed section at the same location after improvements. Sidewalks widened, parking lane eliminated, electric service poles removed and new lighting installed.

Existing section at intersection of Mott Avenue. Narrow sidewalk on the East side (left) has to accommodate a bus stop.

Improved condition at the same location would increase the sidewalk width by forty per cent on both sides. A fixed canopy adds to the street unity on the East side.

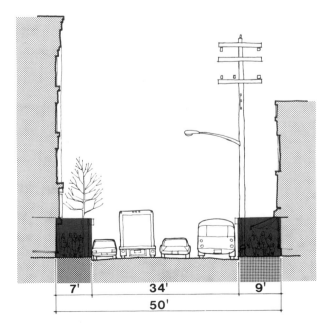

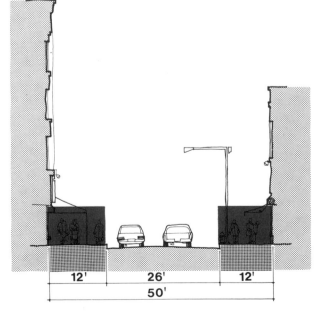

necessarily contribute to retail sales; indeed, they confirm that streetfront parking, when it gets out of control and conflicts with other vehicular movement, can actually deter shoppers and sales.

Many solutions to the park-and-shop problem have been pursued in recent times. These range from pedestrian malls, completely closed to traffic (excepting emergency vehicles, naturally), to those with vehicular access limited to public transportation, to those with total access to vehicles while done in such a way (as proposed at Beach 20th) that the pedestrians are given enough space to interact with each other, a feeling that shoppers typically enjoy.

Nicolett Mall in Minneapolis, for example was once a dismal stretch of downtown commercial and retail establishments, their owners wondering how to compete with the big shopping centers in the suburbs. The traffic flow was finally diverted, but for public buses, minibuses, and emergency vehicles. Landscaping was planted. New paving was put down. The trickle of pedestrians swelled. So did investment in the rehabilitation of buildings in the area of the mall, and the construction of new buildings. The mall cost some $6 million, back in the mid 1960's. The additional private investment spurred by it since has come to over $220 million. In the several years following the opening of the mall, retail sales jumped a yearly average of 14 per cent.

Fulton Mall, in Fresno, California, has six blocks full of fountains, seating areas, playing areas, vine-covered trellises, and shade trees. It is completely free of traffic. Sales are up 20 per cent annually.

The mall in Kalamazoo, Michigan, which has limited vehicular access and which was one of the very first pedestrianization projects in post-war America, was done with limited resources, but resulted in over $30 million of new construction. Business is up 30 per cent annually.

These examples, plus countless others, help to show that merchants and other businessmen need not fear that less parking on the streets outside their front doors will result in reduced business inside. The facts show that the contrary may be true. For large projects or small improvements like Far Rockaway, parking along the street does not always mean more business.

Storefront activities make the difference

Analyzing vehicular movement and the flow of pedestrians on Beach 20th Street, a number of aspects of the street's life became evident. One major influence on circulation was storefront activity. There were restaurants, cafes and fast-food establishments interspersed among clothing, shoe, jewelry, and furniture stores. These storefronts ranged in width from ten to fifty feet along the sidewalk frontage.

The continuity of the stores on both sides of Beach 20th, and their scale, is one of the most attractive qualities about the street, even though vacancies had become a disrupting factor. The designers made a map detailing the variety of activity, and indicated the comparative volumes of pedestrians for each establishment. The needs of the pedestrians, congregating in greater or lesser numbers at various points along the sidewalk, and the kinds of outdoor improvements that might be desirable were identified.

By drawing the elevations of the buildings, the designers and the community were able to study the scale, architectural details, and the physical condition of every building and store. It was thus determined which were in need of painting, repair, or in some cases, thorough restoration. Moreover, this kind of survey was useful to the owners, helping them see the kinds of improvements that could be privately instigated as part of the revitalization process.

The basic physical and spatial continuity of Beach 20th was further studied in this phase. All the buildings, with a single exception, are one to four stories high. Along the east side of the street, all of them are built right up to the lot line; along the west side, they are set slightly back, but the firm edge is nevertheless maintained. The designers discerned that a cohesive treatment would enhance the physical and visual impact of the street. They were also able to see that the mid-block one-story-high commercial buildings might well benefit from a canopy-style metal frame carrying awnings along that side of the street, thus accentuating its continuity. This is an example of how carefully prepared elevations, put together to show the block as a whole, can serve as an invaluable tool for determining what kinds of new features are needed, where they might best be located, and at what height.

The buildings were categorized in terms of the degree to which improvements were necessary. The need for major renovation was evident in those buildings that had been vacated. Their siding, the basic structure of their walls, the window frames and windows, their storefront features, all were seriously deteriorated. Minor rehabilitation was necessary for the rest of the buildings, where loose plaster, peeling paint, falling signs, and built-up grime were the chief problems. Finally, treatment was necessary for a wide assortment of buildings, consisting of cleaning, a paint job here and there, or the redesigning of signs.

The hardware analysis

Consistent with the designers' approach, a map was also prepared showing the location and types of the many physical objects along the street and its sidewalks. It showed the alignment of the sidewalks, store entrances, manhole covers, lighting fixtures, grates, trees, meters, cellar doors, underground utility lines. Random location of such objects may impede pedestrian flow.

As graphic symbols were assigned to these objects, and as these symbols began proliferating and repeating on the maps, it soon became clear that a number of different agencies responsible for all this hardware would eventually have to be involved in any improvement plan.
There were about thirty, including the Department of Highways, which would have to approve such things as the width and materials of the proposed sidewalks, and the Parks Department, responsible for any streetside landscaping and tree planting. The Department of Public.Works and the Bureau of Gas and Electricity would both have decisive roles in reviewing improvements affecting their jurisdictions. The complexity of such agencies and learning how to communicate with them must be consistent, open, and continual from the earliest stages.

This also applies to private companies, like the Long Island Lighting Company, which became a key factor in dealing with the tangle of overhead wires. These, along with the underground lines that some owners had already paid for putting in,

were this company's responsibility. Invited to meetings of the Revitalization Committee, its representatives said that comprehensive relocation of their lines underground would be difficult and costly. Estimates varied from $3,000 to $10,000 for new underground hookups. But the company agreed to provide the service *if* the owners would connect to the new system at their own expense. That expense proved to be $600 per store. Many owners hesitated. Yet without a switch to such a system, widening the sidewalks was going to be impossible. The goal of shaping a more spacious pedestrian shopping street would be marred if even one owner refused to cooperate.

This situation meant presenting several alternatives in such a way that the visual as well as functional ramifications could be easily evaluated. One view presented (the designers' preference) showed the street with the overhead wires replaced completely. Another view showed the street with new, nicer looking poles, but these would have had to be driven six feet into the ground, thus conflicting with the existing underground utilities. One more alternative suggested feeding overhead wires from behind the buildings, in from Beach 19th and Beach 21st, which would at least have gotten rid of the dangling wire on Beach 20th itself. But again, unless a way could be worked out to get *all* the utilities underground, the full sense of visual power and potential of Beach 20th would not be realized.

A course of action

After several late-hour meetings with community representatives and city agencies, a course of action and a plan for Beach 20th Street evolved. This plan consisted of various interrelated elements: the widening of the sidewalks and the resulting realignment of the street; the relocation of the overhead wires underground, thus also eliminating the utility poles; the provision of the parking lot on Beach 19th, with the new pedestrianway leading into Beach 20th; and the installation of the canopy along the entrance to the stores. Encompassing all these elements was the primary objective of creating a *new image* along the street. To this end, the designers proposed brick paving, new lighting, and tree planting.

The paving of the sidewalks with handsome durable bricks would be complemented by new curbstones of split-face granite. The brick would wrap around the corners leading into Beach 20th from Cornaga and Mott, run the length of the block on both sides, continue along the proposed pedestrianway connection with the new parking lot, and cover the surface of an existing traffic island at the Mott intersection. Black and white paving, in a Z-block pattern, would also clearly demarcate all crosswalks, thus cutting down people's propensity to jaywalk.

The proposed streetlights, a high-pressure-sodium kind, would be placed at intervals on both sides of the street, not only complementing the other improvements but also increasing security. A major goal, after all, was to improve both business and social activity during evenings, not just during the daylight hours.

There were problems getting the Bureau of Gas and Electric to go along with the idea of installing a streetlight design that it was unaccustomed to. The Bureau maintained that the city had no stock of that type to replace it when it breaks down, that there were only a few "standard types" that the maintenance division was using anyhow, and that they were hesitant to get into specially designed lights. They were unwilling to use fixtures made by out-of-state manufacturers. This was an example of the nitty-gritty hassles that a hopeful street-saving contingent can encounter. The lighting finally decided on was a special luminary fixture on a 20 foot high light-post made by a regional manufacturer.

As for the canopy proposal, the designers suggested using translucent fiberglass on an aluminum frame. This could be suspended from the first story of the buildings, starting at the north end of the block, continuing southward to the point at midblock where it would turn onto, and run along, the pedestrianway. The canopy would shield shoppers arriving by car, as they walked from the new parking lot into the street. It would add to the visual aspect of shopping by giving the street a more colorful, unified expression. And being translucent, it would allow light to penetrate into the pedestrian areas adjoining the stores. The street would also be enhanced by art work — perhaps a mural, it was suggested, painted right onto the blank wall bordering the pedestrianway.

Trees and benches were to be placed at locations where pedestrians tend to congregate: outside the movie theater on the south side of the street, along the pedestrianway, and on the traffic island. Species of trees would be chosen that are able to survive in an urban situation, and would be protected by decorative metal grates levelled with the sidewalk.

The designers realized that the impact of the widened sidewalks, the canopies, the new paving and landscaping depended on the real test; getting those overhead wires out of sight. The street's total vista had to be fully opened. It was this basic plan, composed of detailed improvements, that provided a basis for the local merchants, business, and government to move ahead.

A strong community commitment

Local businesses and community groups have consistently shown strong commitment to this street and an ability to relate well to the various complex bureaucracies of the city. These bureaucracies responded to this commitment, not only by working together, but also by sponsoring the use of the $300,000 for improving Beach 20th's pedestrian environment.

This attitude has further inspired the community to shoulder continuing responsibilities. Though the groundbreaking for the area-wide improvements, such as those described for Mott Avenue, began in 1976, the challenge of implementation and maintenance for Beach 20th still remains.

The construction of the new parking lot is well underway. A storefront office, manned by a full-time coordinator, was set up to oversee the rehabilitation of the storefronts, including an ongoing cleaning and maintenance program. Merchants agreed to put the remaining overhead utility wires underground. The design and coordinated scheduling of such improvements as the canopy, signs, graphics, and other features have to be finalized. Promotional campaigns have to be initiated to entice new business to relocate to Beach 20th. Finally, advisory services in design and construction are available at the storefront office, to help merchants.

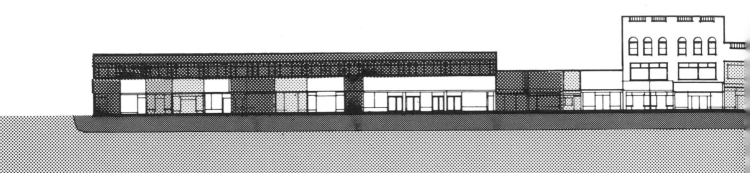

Elevation drawings show existing
conditions of building facades
and where improvements are needed.

Existing storefronts and pedestrian
environment in need of major improvements.

West elevation

Major rehabilitation needed.

Minor repair needed.

Cosmetic treatment needed.

East elevation

Getting the job done

With the $300,000 allocation of 1976, the designers next worked with the community to develop a timetable and an itemized budget. The hope was that the work could begin in the spring of 1977, starting with the construction of the new parking lot and pedestrianway.

Almost everything was in place. A site-selection committee was working to secure the parcel on Beach 19th where the lot would go. The Department of Highways was about to prepare working drawings for the improvements along Beach 20th itself. The Long Island Lighting Company was to get copies of these drawings to clear the way for the new underground utility system. The City's Corporate Counsel was clearing the use of the community development funds for the improvement of privately owned building facades. The Bureau of Gas and Electric Company agreed to pay for the new decorative lights that had been proposed along the street and pedestrianway, provided the community would provide upkeep and new bulbs. All these wheels were in motion. However, the hopes for a spring deadline were not to be realized so soon.

Following the earlier stages of the revitalization process leading up to this juncture, a period of decline followed, throwing the process into a serious spasm. The social structure of the neighborhood changed, with more low-income groups replacing the middle-income residents, many of whom had been solidly behind the revitalization. Out of the some sixty stores along this block, about thirty had already been left vacant. The beginnings of construction of the physical improvement along the street hastened this process. It is, therefore, not incidental to such strategy that the first phase of implementation — addressing the need for that parking lot, as well as improvements on the other adjacent street — had led to a physically destructive attitude. Instead of lifting morale and vision, this work created environmental problems such as noise and pollution. At the time the physical improvement implementation began to take place, new youth gangs and arsonists moved in, causing serious concern along Beach 20th Street, depressing the spirits of the merchants along the street. Within the following three

Above: Existing conditions of Beach 20th Street; Opposite: New improved street with wider sidewalks, decorative pavement, refurbished storefronts and new lighting fixtures will be inviting for both shopper and storeowner.

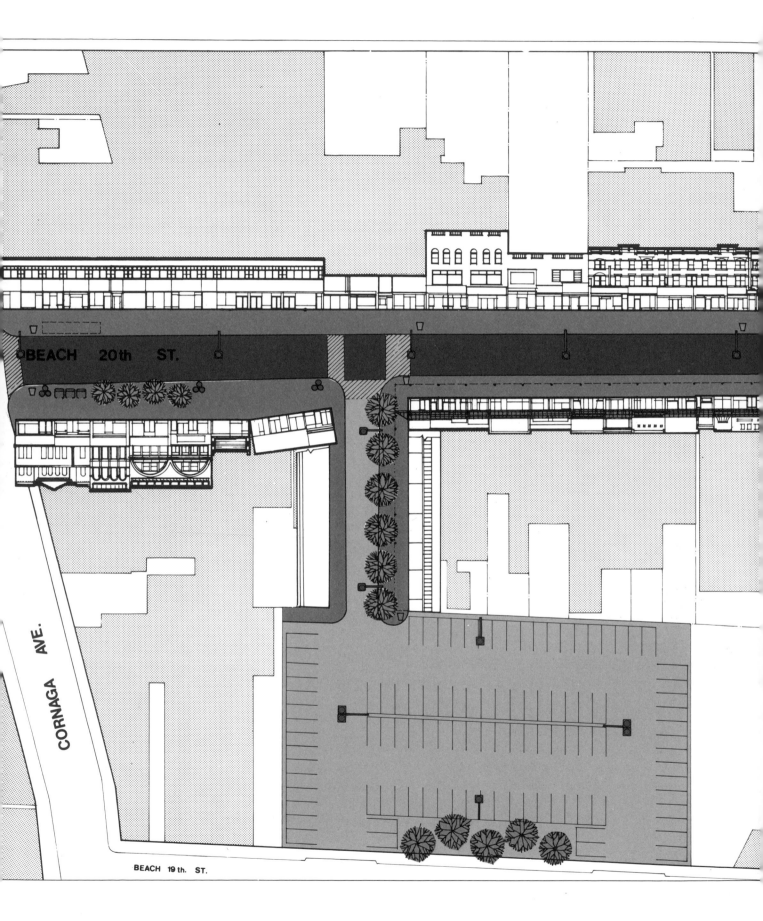

BEACH 20th ST.

CORNAGA AVE.

BEACH 19th ST.

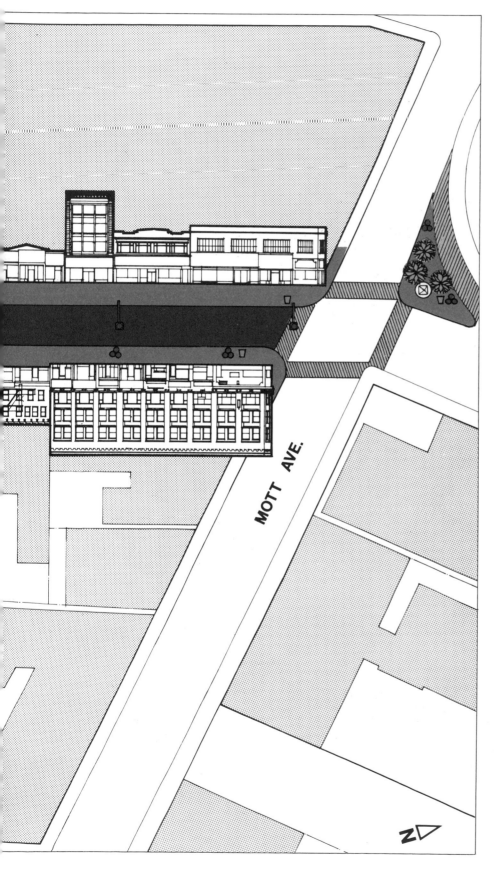

The proposed plan

Proposed plan includes:
A new parking lot
A pedestrian passage to parking lot
Elimination of meter parking
Cleaning of facades
Upgrading of the storefronts
Elimination of electric poles
Replacement street lights
Installing pedestrian lights
Relocation of street trees
Widening of sidewalks
Repaving of sidewalks
Paving of pedestrian crossing
Improvement of traffic island
Artwork on blank walls

View of street before and after improvement looking south.

View of street before and after improvement at south east corner.

to four months, it was hard to tell whether the revitalized process was just going through a rough period, or whether it was really in serious, irreversible jeopardy.

The task force in the city did not abandon their resolve to fight. The City Planning Department, for its part, responded to this new reality by developing a socially oriented program to rehabilitate housing in the area, and to provide more social service. A reevaluation of the improvements on the newly devastated area was undertaken.

As the social problems were revealed, several weaknesses in the process became apparent. The original community participants did not have enough representatives from among the building owners and merchants along the street. There had been representation, to be sure, and as we have noted, it was strong and outspoken. But this turned out to be insufficient. Furthermore, the participants were predominantly of an institutional nature, such as the Jewish Federation Group, and did not represent other ethnic groups in the area. It is now clear that a better balance between merchants and various institutional interests would have been beneficial.

This means the need for a lot more education of the new merchants to the benefits of revitalization. This is made all the more urgent because, of the merchants now along Beach 20th, only 25 per cent were there at the beginning of the revitalization process. The other 75 per cent were new. Many of them lease their space as opposed to owning it outright. This, in turn, brought into question the nature and the depth of commitment. Realizing this problem, a major effort was begun by the task force to include more merchants and owners in order to hasten improvements right along the street itself, and produce a tangible, plan for the street improvement.

The lessons learned have begun to bear fruit. New merchants are coming to Beach 20th; additional groups are getting involved. And today the basic work is underway. An additional $200,000 has been allocated for a second pedestrian connection from Beach 20th to Beach 21st. All but one store owner has agreed to connect with the new utility system. While the canopy along the storefronts is not going to go ahead for a while,

the paving is proceeding apace. And not far back in the minds of everyone is the prospect of approval by the state legislature to permit casinos in New York which may include Far Rockaway, out by the water. Certainly this would have a major impact on Beach 20th, as it would on the economic outlook of the area as a whole.

Beach 20th is a borderline situation now, the retail core of a declining, troubled, but determined community. The very ability of the street to rejuvenate itself, to reverse these negative changes, has been in question. But if that rejuvenation is going to occur, if the reversal is to take place, all the steps that have been taken suggest that *this* street can be the generator for improving the neighborhood as a whole. Certainly the effort is beginning to unify diverse groups and interests, despite all the obstacles. These steps may seem like small victories towards a new image, but as we have emphasized throughout, street improvements and urban revitalization realistically occur one step at a time to gradually provide a total, well coordinated plan.

There is an important lesson here in the Far Rockaway experience. Even when unsuspected crises occur, even when new economic or social groups move in, comprehensive and coordinated planning can keep the pieces intact and sustain a community's momentum toward putting them together. While the population, impulses, and priorities may change, the new Beach 20th Street will serve its neighbors in the same supportive, familiar way as the original Beach 20th Street served its own.

LONG TERM IMPLEMENTATION: TOOLS FOR THE FUTURE

WHAT IS LONG TERM IMPLEMENTATION?

Throughout, this book has emphasized making feasible, affordable, short-term improvements to your street. These improvements can become a framework for long-term implementation. There are a number of tools available to you to reinforce your immediate improvements into a more far-reaching future plan — tools such as zoning laws, facade easements, tax abatements, and your community's administrative codes.

By now you have the advantage of evaluating the temporary actions and their success. A month-long street-closing program, for example, could provide clues to what a more permanent traffic plan should be. Moreover, this understanding will help you envision immediate short-term improvements as practical, sturdy foundation stones for the later and more extensive stages of your street's environment. The long-term tools might seem technical at times, but a basic understanding of them will be a key to helping you in implementing your plans for future change.

A better knowledge of long-range-planning techniques will permit you to utilize creative approaches in adapting these land-use tools to your street's specific needs. For example, if your street is in a preservation district and a new building is planned for construction that does not conform to the character of the district, you must know what tools will permit you to stop the project or instead relate it to the surrounding buildings. Or else in your pedestrian plan, you may want to limit truck entrances. In such a case, it will be helpful for you to know that, in New York, high-density-residential areas limit curb cuts to one per building, and curb cuts are not permitted at all along major retail streets such as Fifth Avenue, Madison Avenue, and Mulberry Street.

These implementation tools may not have been originally created for street-improvement projects; in fact, they address general land-use issues, and they fall into two categories. The first category is mandatory. In which case they may be included within the zoning ordinance. Sometimes they are included within administrative codes. Some tools are voluntary, and are written in the form of design-and-development guidelines. Voluntary tools don't have the enforcement strength of mandates and do not hold in courts, yet they are free of bureaucratic interference and allow for flexibility in design. What often gives them more meaning are the incentives by which cities attempt to engage the interest of developers. In exchange for such options as additional density or coverage, the city entices the developer to provide amenities such as covered pedestrian spaces, parks, and, in New York, even theaters.

Comprehensive Planning

The most traditional planning tool is the master plan. A master plan is basically a comprehensive long-range document, illustrated with maps. It depicts elements of the physical environment, and is the official guide for controlling present and future land use. A land-use map specifies the kind of use (whether the land has been developed as residential or commercial), the location of the uses (where roads, housing, and factories are located), the intensity of the use permitted (high-rise vis-`a-vis low-rise, the number of people per acre, the volume and coverage allowed on a piece of property, and where built-up areas are located as opposed to open space). The master plan also includes components of social and cultural importance, in varying detail.

While it is essential to have a plan—whether a large one for an entire city or, as in your case, of a street—recently, criticism has been mounting as to the merits and effectiveness of such a document. A number of cities have shelved the master plan, as New York did right after its preparation in 1969. The New York master plan has been replaced by a series of community miniplans. This decline of the popularity of the master plan is due to a number of major changes affecting land-use planning, today, i.e. people becoming more transient, scarcer energy, changing transportation needs, a slowdown in the economy, and recognition of the value of older buildings. All these factors occurred too fast to become part of a stamped "master plan." For example, a building that would be saved today for its historical merit might have been torn down only ten years ago. Not only does the traditional master plan allow for little flexibility, but it does not reflect the present trend of community advocacy and participation. Also, when a master plan is in place, it is extremely tedious and time-consuming to have to deal with the bureaucracy involved in change. The demapping of a street in New York City, for example, takes a minimum of six months to a more likely maximum of two years.

The fact is that the master planning of a city has proven to be no panacea. No "official thinking" during one year or decade, however eloquently it is expressed, can anticipate all of the diverse dynamics at work in shaping cities. This is not to say that for your street comprehensive planning is not good; it is to say that once a miniplan is in place, indicating the major land use factors such as densities and the location of primary paths for cars and pedestrians, other tools, such as performance standards, are available to allow for more flexibility and the incorporation of new ways of life. For instance, alternate transportation methods may require bicycle lanes along your street; your master plan must accommodate a change in your street's right-of-way. You must strike a balance between how much you include in your master plan and how much you leave open to allow for the unpredictable future.

Land Acquisition

Any improvement in your street requires the cooperation of the owners along the street. With private owners, you will need to consider a variety of interests. In the case of public ownership or control, you may have a greater flexibility in making improvements. Therefore, the ways in which land is bought, controlled, and used are basic to understanding how streets change. Two common methods of land acquisition are urban renewal and development corporations.

Urban Renewal: Urban renewal is a legislative tool that emerged from the Federal Housing Act of 1949, whose goal was to secure a decent roof for every American and to eliminate urban blight. Such legislation provides funds for cities to acquire land even without the consent of the owner. In cities of over 500,000 people, it effectively extends the power of eminent domain through the municipality to an approved developer to carry out a plan. The objective of such a plan has to be in accordance with the public purpose set.

Although originally well intentioned, urban renewal legislation has resulted in some unfortunate consequences. For many years following the 1949 act, urban renewal automatically meant demolishing old housing, stores, and institutions, to "free" the land which often was in the downtown centers of our cities. Through the process of demolition, properties on the edges of these urban renewal areas were neglected, frequently causing greater blight and despair. When built, the new developments were often massive concrete buildings, like fortresses surrounded by parking lots. In contrast, urban renewal has rejuvenated whole cities, as the successes of New Haven and Boston demonstrate.

Urban Renewal
Boston

Today, urban renewal as a tool has become more versatile. Besides the power to acquire land, it encompasses, among others, land-code-enforcement provisions for allowing the restoration of architecturally significant buildings and, in effect, has become a minimaster plan. In addition, urban renewal funding can be used for small-scale improvements; in Savannah, Georgia, new sidewalks and lighting were paid for by urban renewal funds.

It is important to know whether your street is part of an official urban renewal area. If it is, certain parcels along your street may be subject to the guidelines and requirements of the urban renewal plan for that district. In such a case, you may choose to incorporate your own ideas into the plan and use it as your implementation tool.

Local Development Corporations: A local development corporation is a business or not-for-profit corporation formed to stimulate and implement economic development in a particular community. An LDC is formed in cases where little incentive exists for a private developer. In communities that do not have sufficient market potential to attract private developers, LDC often becomes the developer of last resort. Its own special powers are limited by its mandate, having access to the greater powers of the city, such as the ability to borrow low-cost money. It can also provide low-interest, long-term financing, and real-estate-tax exemptions but does not include powers of condemnation for land acquisition, which are given to an urban redevelopment corporation.

The major advantage in forming an LDC is to have greater access to Small Business Administration Loans, Economic Development Action Grants, and other such public financing.

Under New York State law, the development power of an LDC includes the ability to purchase or lease city property without public bidding. Also, LDC is an additional and alternate method of incorporation of not-for-profit corporations, and it is established with the intentions of operating for ''exclusively charitable or public purposes.'' It shares several similarities with a private corporation, with the major exception of its tax-exempt status. The formation of a local development plan has to be approved by the local

and state legislatures in order to assume its public purpose and its powers that are more substantial than those of a private developer.

The most likely roles for an LDC in New York City are as a sponsor and as a vehicle for the private sector to assist projects that benefit the public. As such, its major function is to provide a conveyance to channel city-owned property to the private developer or business, and to take the initiative for obtaining community approvals. In return for this assistance, the LDC can often receive some of the financial benefit from the developer to be used for other economic activities within the community. Developers are often willing to provide LDC sponsors with a share of tax shelter sale returns, cash flow, and sometimes, proceeds from refinancing. On the other hand, the developer will want to retain operating control of the project and will rarely give the LDC any review power over its operations.

Theatre Row
42nd St.
New York City

The Forty-second Street Local Development Corporation in New York is a good example of an owner/developer structure of an LDC as it applies to a street. Established in 1976, when there was little interest in the area, the LDC was created to plan the renewal of the Eighth to Twelfth Avenue blocks on Forty-second Street. The corporation is now a private, not-for-profit, tax-exempt LDC, and its current mandate involves planning for all of Forty-second Street. The corporation holds a one-dollar per-year lease with the city on the city-owned properties involved. The corporation has received funding from diverse sources for different phases of their proposals; some of these include Urban Development Block Grants for street improvements, a grant from a private foundation to study transportation methods, a permanent mortgage from the

Bowery Savings Bank, and an Urban Development Action Grant from HUD for the rehabilitation of theaters along the street. Under the expert direction of Fred Papert, its president, the first phase of this project succeeded in converting five derelict tenements into five renovated Off-Broadway theaters with a total of ten floors of rehearsal and office space. Using the mechanism of an LDC, the Forty-second Street LDC with distinguished board members has reversed the decline of West Forty second Street and encouraged both government and private developers to reinvest in the area.

A similar function to New York's LDC is performed by the Dayton, Ohio City-Wide Development Corporation and Oregon's Portland Development Commission. PDC was created in 1958 by the city's voters in a referendum to amend the City Charter. It was done at the suggestion of the Mayor's Advisory Committee on Urban Renewal, as a way to enact the state's urban renewal laws. Now, in operation over twenty years, the Development Commission performs all functions of the city relating to blight clearance, urban renewal, and development.

"PDC develops urban renewal plans, acquires properties, relocates persons displaced by project activities, assists in the rehabilitation of homes and buildings, and contracts for the design and construction of public improvements. The Development Commission is also authorized to promote industrial growth and the expansion of business in and near the city. To carry out these responsibilities, PDC has the authority to acquire, develop, sell or lease property. It may borrow money on the private market or accept donations. PDC also receives funds through the city from the Federal Housing and Community Development Block Grant Program for use in housing and neighborhood revitalization efforts."

LDCs are widely used across the country in large and small cities alike. They often expedite implementation of a plan because they approach a project in a businesslike manner and therefore involve less red tape than government agencies. For your street, the LDC may be just the right management framework you need to implement your plans. Use an existing local authority, if one is available; otherwise you may want to form your own.

TRADITIONAL ZONING

Your streetscape and your city skyline are more a reflection of zoning laws than the result of sheer aesthetics. The prime purpose of zoning, as defined by the first such ordinance in America (New York's in 1916), is to protect the public by regulating land use. This pioneering measure limited the size and shape of buildings, designated areas for parks and open spaces, regulated parking areas, and controlled population densities. It also carved the city into zones separating incompatible uses such as manufacturing, retail, and residential areas from each other. Thus, the public interest, health, and safety were protected. Minimum standards for admitting light and air were established, providing "setbacks" in buildings above a certain height, thereby allowing light and air to other buildings as well as onto the streets and sidewalks, making them more sunny and pleasant. These regulations have been applied to individual parcels on a lot-by-lot basis.

Building Setbacks
Defined by Zoning

Today, traditional zoning has become an accepted measure in most cities and is recognized as a legally valid extension of the government's role to police and promote the public's well-being. Yet in the past ten to fifteen years, the application of zoning has broadened dramatically. Instead of using zoning as a "negative" tool specifying what not to do, zoning is being used today as a creative mechanism, addressing a wide range of planning goals. These include incentives to extract public amenities and preserve neighborhoods, while at the same time providing benefits to the developer.

New York City has been a leader in the use of incentive zoning, beginning in the mid-1960's, just as it was a pioneer in 1916. The change is essentially this: zoning, which began as regulations to restrict, has now been utilized to enrich; zoning, which began with an emphasis on individual lots, has been expanded as a framework to define and lend distinction to the special qualities of street and districts; zoning, originally challenged in the courts as a confiscation of property rights, has extended its power to include incentives to provide pedestrian amenities and to preserve landmarks, thus encouraging a more humane and livable environment.

Traditional zoning, taken to its extreme, ended up isolating activities from each other and destroying the mixture and vitality in neighborhoods. They created sterile downtown areas. Dissatisfaction with wasted infrastructure and social environments has led to a new approach of "mix-use zoning" that encourages a better relationship between transportation, housing, and the working environment. So today, on your street, the location of a residential apartment above a mom-and-pop store may conform to zoning regulations after all.

While most large cities use their zoning as their land-use regulatory tool, some cities may use an administrative code to effect their planning. In New York City, both an administrative code and a zoning resolution are in effect. The zoning is the more stringent tool; the administrative code allows for more flexibility. On your own street, make sure that you are familiar with the powers of both if they are available to you.

As dry, distant, and legalistic as the terms "zoning" and "administrative code" seem, they may be the most pervasive forces at work shaping the physical environment.

In your exploration of available mechanisms for changing your street, you may need a fundamental knowledge of some basic zoning terminology. Here are a number of commonly used terms:

Floor Area Ratio

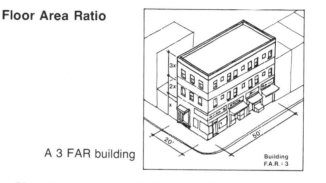

A 3 FAR building

Usually written as FAR, it is a factor by which building bulk is measured in relation to the size of a lot. For example, on a site of one thousand square feet with a floor area ratio of three, three thousand square feet of building floor space are allowed.

Lot-by-Lot

San Francisco

In the traditional zoning approach, regulations about density, bulk, site coverage, setbacks, open space, and parking have customarily been geared to individual parcels. This lot-by-lot approach does provide for light and air around a specific site, but does not always address the planning issues of an integrated street or a whole environment. For instance, the open space around a single building may provide light and air to the building but can become a "leftover" space which breaks the existing street wall and interrupts the retail continuity from one store to another. Therefore, today's approach to zoning on a lot-by-lot basis has been expanded to special districts and area planning that are not merely limited to benefiting the single lot but also address the problems of a total environment.

Conforming and Nonconforming Uses

A conforming use is one that falls within the range of activities for which a zoning type has been designated. A nonconforming use is, conversely, one that intrudes upon that range. For instance, industrial and mercantile functions are often noxious and unhealthy neighbors when adjacent to residential and retail areas. Lately, zoning has become less restrictive in terms of mixed use, allowing the integration of a variety of uses within specific areas or even within a single building. New performing standards—the recognition of the importance of mixed-use for the vitality of the street, the desire to maximize the existing infrastructure, and the new awareness of the effectiveness of performing standards—have made many non-conforming uses obsolete (for example, the Soho District in New York permits artists' residences and manufacturing uses within the same building).

As-of-Right Vis-à-Vis Special Permit

An as-of-right building is, quite simply, one that conforms to the regulations of the zoning code and does not require variances from any regulatory body.

A special permit, however, is required in cases where the zoning mandates that some review body be involved in the project's approval process. A special permit is also mandated when a developer is seeking a change in size, bulk, density, parking areas, or any other uses beyond the permitted regulations under the zoning code. While a special permit often allows for community input, it is not a favorite tool of private developers since it is time-consuming and subject to discretionary action.

Performance Standards

Performance standards have been commonly used in environmental legislation applying to clean air, water, and noise. Lately, they have been extended to include land-use issues. Land-use performance standards evaluate specific issues such as density, height, air, and light based on superior quality performance. They are rated with respect to their performance in a certain area rather than on the traditional regulations. Conventional rules are based on rigid standards quantifying the amount of densities, height measurements, and building volumes. A performance standard, for example, may call for providing a view from every window of a residential building instead of mandating the size of a window or a precise angle view from every location.

Cincinnati Hillside

Cincinnati's Hillside Development Guidelines establish performance standards respecting the maintenance of the hill's shapes and contours, thus preserving views and relating new building heights to their environment.

Rather than assign the traditional quantitative measurements regarding housing, the housing quality standards of New York City attempt to improve quality through performance standards. The basis of the system is dependent on four categories of performance: Recreation Space, Security and Safety, Building Interior, and Neighborhood Impact. Each of the categories has guidelines with a point system assigned to determine fulfillment of the spirit of the legislation. The program for Recreation Space, for example, encourages the creation of distinct outdoor areas that reflect the needs of the tenant population, with separate facilities for adult-use activities, children's play areas, space for mixed use rather than the conventional way of defining open space as a measurement of a percentage of open area to built-up area.

In Security and Safety, the performance standards call for discouraging crime and vandalism by opening up public areas to maximum visual surveillance by using large clear-glass windows in places such as elevator entrances, lobbies, and corridors, thereby making it easier for occupants to recognize their neighbors and identify outsiders. Instead of demanding enclosed high walls and fences in public areas, this system encourages visibility and added personnel for better security.

In the Building Interior program, the housing quality standards encourage large, sunny, and well-ventilated rooms and bonus cross-ventilation, recessed balconies, natural light in corridors, and bulk-storage space within the units. This is obviously a breakthrough in traditional housing requirements that mandate minimum sizes of rooms.

The Neighborhood Impact section is designed to ensure continuity with, and sensitivity to, the character of the existing neighborhood. For example, for buildings located on a vacant lot between two existing structures, a typical performance standard can state that "the building must relate to the buildings next to it." Such a requirement is less strict than calling for cornices to align and allows for more adaptable and innovative design relationships.

Performance standards may be an attractive tool to use for your street's protection; however, you should know that the enforcement of these standards is evaluated on a case-by-case basis and, therefore, requires hiring more professionals.

CREATIVE ZONING

Creative zoning is an approach which provides innovative tools to address new planning concepts. It expands traditional zoning to include the techniques of the special district. It adds definitions to the zoning ordinance such as pedestrian amenities. It uses zoning power to preserve existing buildings and to encourage environmental awareness, and it extends its jurisdiction from regulating land use within the building line to amenities along the street. While not necessarily less restrictive, creative zoning provides a variety of new tools that could be tailored to your specific needs as you launch your street improvement program.

Incentive Zoning

Incentive zoning is a measure by which a developer is granted a benefit in the form of additional density of larger coverage, in exchange for providing public amenities. In New York City, the 1961 revised zoning law introduced the first incentive zoning provisions that encouraged developers to provide open space and arcades at ground level in return for increased density up to 20 per cent above the basic density allowed by

law. Since then, incentive zoning has been expanded to include through-block arcades, covered pedestrian spaces, and the preservation of landmarks.

Special Districts

The unique character of your street can be protected and accentuated if the street is designated as a special district. In essence, it is a legal plan pioneered in New York City, and now working in a number of others, that identifies the theme of a street — its physical mix of activities, its social and cultural texture — and then insures its preservation. The regulations for a special zoning district require drawing up a detailed plan of the area, showing its special uses and particular physical characteristics along with a strong visual sense of what should be done to reinforce and preserve them.

If your street is located on or near a waterfront, for example, then you may want to maintain views of the water. Within a special district, regulations could be put into effect whereby lines of sight of a specified width must be maintained, thus precluding any development that might infringe upon these vistas. To take another example, if your street has an arcade which connects buildings, special district regulations could guarantee that a new building include an arcade as well.

The kind of cohesiveness and continuity described here cannot be ensured by zoning measures that are administered on a building-by-building basis. Yet, it can be achieved by picking up on the strongest theme that a district and its streets have, and incorporating it into a legislative program.

This was the case when New York introduced the concept with the Special Theater District. There zoning incentives were appropriately tailored to encourage developers to include theaters in their new buildings in exchange for additional office floor space. This measure was intended to preserve the unique enclave of theaters in the Broadway area, in danger of demolition in the face of the growing development of new office buildings. It was also the case with the Fifth Avenue Special District, which was conceived to strengthen the spirited retail life by mandating small shops and limiting banks and travel agencies on the ground level along that famous street.

The Atlantic Avenue Special District in Brooklyn is preserving three- and four-story buildings with their ground-level shops. Here the legislation sets guidelines for renovating and altering noteworthy buildings and provides for signage controls for storefronts. These controls mandate the use of size and color that relate to the inherent beauty of the buildings. Similarly, the Special Madison Avenue Preservation District promotes the lively, diverse commercial and retail charm of that Manhattan street by stipulating that the first stories be used only for small boutiques. The district also includes a height limitation to reduce its density and improve the penetration of sunlight to the street.

The controls of the special district define planning objectives of a specified area and, in most cases, mandate related amenities on individual parcels in accordance with such a framework. Another innovative way to use the special district technique is in a situation where an amenity exists within the district, such as a park or a major public building. A fund to improve such an amenity

Madison Ave. Special District, New York City

can be formed directing the individual lot improvement to one amenity.

One example is the Park Improvement District along upper Fifth and Park avenues' residential areas in New York. There the owners are required to provide money through a special fund for the improvement of that portion of Central Park located opposite their buildings. The objective of this special district is to improve the existing open space rather than to add plazas around the buildings, thereby creating redundant amenities opposite a park. Instead the strong walls of the streets at the edge of the park and opposite the Park Avenue malls, are maintained. Special districts as a legal tool are thus useful whether you want to encourage a new look or use on your street, or whether you want to protect its physical continuity and scale.

Zoning for Street Amenities

Tree Planting in New York City

Tree Planting: While zoning can deal with large parcels of land, it can deal with the smallest scale of amenity as well. Your zoning might include, for instance, provisions for the planting of trees —specifying the distance between them, their caliper, and even the depth of the soil.

Amenities Required in New York Plazas

There are some possible problems, however. In New York, for instance, it was learned that most trees do not survive in planters. You will also want to double-check which species are particularly fit for your environment. Make sure they are hardy enough, and then pick out the most attractive one as a unifying element for your street. You may choose a flowering tree or an evergreen, depending on the geographical area of your street.

In New York, regulations of trees varies from one special district to another, although they are mandated for all high-density residential areas. If you decide to seek a similar provision for your street, be sure to check the underground utilities so that there will be no interference caused by the roots of the trees. Also, don't make a blanket provision for trees unless there is plenty of pedestrian room on the sidewalks. All in all, trees add a lot more to a street than just charm and good looks. They can serve as a buffer against noise, promote clean air, and soften the atmosphere on the street in contrast to the hard edges of the buildings. Symbolically as well as physically, trees can instill a visual rhythm to the street, or provide a border between your commercial strip and a historic district, or separate pedestrians from parking lots.

Public Open Space: The introduction of amenities through zoning can include standards for the location and features of public spaces. As pointed out earlier, the 1961 revision of New York City's zoning law placed great emphasis on plazas — giving floor area bonuses to developers in return for urban open space. This turned out to be an attractive provision to developers, but resulted in a plethora of plaza space which disrupted the continuity of shops along retail streets. Moreover, the plazas were often barren, devoid of any real

human appeal. A recent revision of the legislation relating to public open space has reversed this trend by placing great importance on the quality of these spaces. Highly specific in its requirements, it is definitely oriented toward people. For example, all plaza spaces around new buildings have to be located on the side of the building or lot that receives the most sunlight. Such a provision must, of course, be tailored to your own climate. In very hot places like New Mexico, you may want to put the premium on places that offer shade; in extremely cold places like Minnesota, you may want to encourage public spaces, like the IDS Center in Minneapolis, which are covered, skylighted, and protected from the harsher winter months. Try to relate and employ the qualities of your public spaces to local conditions, and always offer features and activities that will encourage people to enjoy their streets and their urban spaces.

The range and detail of specific amenities within the space can vary from being very detailed to more general. One provision requires the elevation of the open space to be at the same elevation as the sidewalk in order to facilitate access for the handicapped. Others require the placement of a specific number of seats, litter receptacles, and artwork. Some of the amenities, such as bicycle racks and water fountains, are mandatory, while additional trees, fountains, and artwork are left to the discretion of the owner. These improvements are given by the private builder in exchange for permission from the city to add additional floor area to the building in question.

Let's assume that a new building is going up in an area where you had anticipated the need for seating and related pedestrian comforts. You may want to develop legislation for your street in ad-

Greenacre Park
New York City

vance, taking precaution against the eventuality of a parking lot in that spot. In your rules for that site, you may want to require the developer to provide trees and benches, to pave the front of his building in accordance with the street's revitalization theme, or else you may want to mandate a particular kind of curbstone which would lend a further unity. If your street is part of a special district, or an official historic area, you may well be in a position to be legally even more restrictive in defining the range of material and colors.

Sidewalk Cafes: Cafes can enhance the attractiveness and vitality of your street and add to the total quality of life in your neighborhood. In a recent study of New York's two hundred new sidewalk cafes, it was noted that while cafes contributed activity and ambience to the streets, they also produced some problems. Many cafes in inappropriate locations became obstructions to pedestrians and caused congestion in high-density areas. Others were unattractive: rather than adding to their settings, they were disharmonious elements on the street.

The Museum Cafe
New York City

Since cafes are owned by private enterprises, yet use the public sidewalks, public regulation of sidewalk cafes is required in order to protect the public's rights and safety as well as to encourage good design. If you want to allow a sidewalk cafe along your street, make sure the location of the sidewalk cafe is not in an overcrowded area. Also, allow for a minimum sidewalk width needed to accommodate both the cafe and pedestrians comfortably after the cafe is built. Pay special attention to the spatial requirements at corners and transportation-gathering areas.

A sidewalk cafe can be unenclosed or covered by glass. In warm climates, like that in Southern California, cafes can be open to the sky, deco-

rated with attractive awnings, umbrellas, or potted plants. In areas where protection from inclement weather is desirable, enclosed cafes are possible. In such places, a cafe in a glass pavilion can be lovely—transparent and light. If you think you have an enforcement procedure as good as the one in Paris, use their rule of removing the windows in the summertime. In your design guidelines, minimize the proportion of solid structure. While you may permit glass to be polarized for sun control, be careful not to allow the use of dark glass which obscures the interior. Discourage the use of heavy draperies, tiny windows, painted glass, and drawn venetian blinds which destroy one of the essential features of cafes—direct visual communication between the person who sips espresso in the cafe and the pedestrian along the street.

A good rule of thumb is that the best cafes are those built at the same level as the sidewalk. Limit the change of grade between the cafe and the sidewalk, and avoid steps or elevated construction which tend to isolate the cafe from the sidewalk.

The New York sidewalk cafe guidelines limit the size of signs, establish maximum height for the cafe structure, and confine uses to food services only. Along your street, you may not need to go to such detail to achieve a joyful environment and to entice an owner to follow your wish. Above all, don't forget, a cafe is not a heavy, boxlike construction sticking out of a building onto the sidewalk, but a place where people can sit leisurely and watch others pass by.

Zoning Influences Retail Use

Zoning, in the traditional sense, separated residential, commercial, and manufacturing uses, fencing them off from each other, often causing such inconveniences as locating shops miles away from residential areas. However, on your street, you may want to encourage stores on the ground level of the buildings, with a mix of offices or apartments up above.

Many economic and social forces have modified the old-time qualities of the small retail street. These forces often replaced the small grocery with a big bank, the boutique with a department store, or a favorite restaurant with a fast-food outlet. While zoning measures, however enlightened, cannot be depended upon to bring back the grocery store, they can help you attract the more humanly scaled stores and maintain those establishments that remain along your street. A special district designation could differentiate your street from others, giving it a distinctive appeal by encouraging a mix of activities at many hours of the day and night.

Within your special district, you could include a use-group listing, outlining those uses which you want to preserve. Assuming that you want to spur as much around-the-clock activity as possible (always beneficial for a retail-street environment), you would want to eliminate from your use group large banks, funeral parlors, insurance companies, and other limited-hours-per-day operations.

Scribner Bookstore
New York City

In the case of the Fifth Avenue Special District in New York, a use group includes art galleries, bookstores, and local retail establishments. What was not wanted along the street were activities like banks or big airline ticket offices which occupy stretches of window frontage along the sidewalk and "turn off" at five or six in the afternoon, leaving nothing for pedestrians to look at inside but a lot of empty counters and silent computer terminals. These inactive uses were therefore limited in the use group to occupy only 10 per cent of the frontage. The essential concept is to determine those use groups that will most handsomely preserve the character of your street and to eliminate uses that don't add to the street's vitality.

By the same token, you may not want to exclude any uses at all, but prefer limiting the size of the frontage of each establishment to maintain the small-store quality and the variety of stores

along your street. You may do it by allowing a frontage of not more than twenty feet, or by limiting the number of stores on each block. Use-group listing and limited frontage per store are legal tools to help you maintain the feeling of small, personal boutiques with familiar faces.

The exclusion or limitation of fast-food outlets or adult-entertainment places becomes more complicated and can be challenged on the grounds of violation of both the First and Fourteenth Amendments which protect the freedom of speech and guarantee equal right under the law.

In regard to the concentration of fast-food stores, which occasionally become synonymous with trash and garish signs, the number of such establishments can be controlled through a use group only if all food establishments, even the most elegant restaurants, are also excluded. Otherwise, the best way to discourage these uses is to limit sign sizes and curb cuts as was done in Eugene, Oregon. Obviously, such measures will not be popular with food establishments if they depend on motorists for their business.

As to adult uses, you can use zoning laws to control the permissible distance between such places and thereby prevent a concentration of undesirable spots. Any action to prevent the influx of pornographic operations will affect your community. If you want to exclude pornography from a street, you ought to be aware of alternate methods that are being tried around the country which don't challenge the Constitution. Even if your street does not have pornographic establishments on it directly, knowing what your options are may help you to influence your city's policy on that complex matter.

There are two major ways to fight these eyesores using zoning measures. The first way is to establish a red light district, as in Boston, concentrating pornographic uses in one area. The second, and completely opposite, is to disperse it, as was done in Detroit and New York. The truth is, of course, that neither method is totally effective.

In Boston, while the famous (or infamous) Scollay Square area was cleared of its assorted adult-use hangouts, starting in the 1950s, and was turned into a magnificent civic center district, no real concerted effort was made to prevent the reconcentration of such uses. Instead, by the mid-

1960s, a new area, dubbed the "Combat Zone," had begun to form not far from Boston's central business district. By the mid-1970s, it had become the center for topless bars and cabarets, adult movie theaters, pinball parlors, and adult bookstores. In an effort to keep the porno plague from spreading to other vulnerable areas, the "Zone" was designated as "the most logical place" for the "red light" district of Boston. By containing adult uses in one area, it was expected that Boston could more readily police these uses and substantially prevent them from having a blighting effect on the rest of the city. The thinking went further. If Boston could police the area, people wishing to avoid it could easily do so. While achieving the goal of containment, the results are debatable. Some claim that intensification of the problem and more serious abuses went hand in hand with greater enforcement problems. Others claim that what had been discreetly degenerate became openly so.

In contrast to Boston's experience, Detroit, bulldozing its skid-row district in 1962, enacted a zoning ordinance that placed strict limits of both location and concentration on specified-land uses ordinarily found in run-down sections; i.e., pornographic uses had to be located at least a thousand feet apart. Initially it was successful in preventing reconcentration, but in the early 1970s the number of such places began to proliferate again. In a landmark legal case, Detroit's "restrictive" measure was challenged, and in mid-1976, the Supreme Court sustained Detroit's position toward restricting establishments dealing with pornography, whether movie theaters, peep shows, or bookstores.

New York City's attempt to control pornography must be viewed in a different context. In 1955, there were nine adult uses in the city; in 1976, there were 245. With a high concentration of pornography in Times Square and the theater district, new businesses and development kept away and the quality of the area suffered physical decay. After the landmark Supreme Court decision in Detroit, and after a comprehensive study of land-use patterns in the city, New York City prepared zoning recommendations to disperse and limit adult uses. The legislative form of these recommendations was enacted in 1978 and was closely modeled on Detroit's. Depending on your situation, you may want to encourage legislation to disperse uses along your street, like Detroit did, or else influence your government to create a red light district like the one in Boston, which will eventually redirect those uses away from your street.

Zoning Around Transportation Nodes

Zoning can be an effective tool for easing congestion around transportation centers, where people get on or off subways or buses in heavy numbers. In New York, zoning legislation was designed to improve transit facilities through joint development with the private property owners around the stations of the proposed Second Avenue Subway line. Instead of relying on the all-too-familiar hassle of crowded mid-sidewalk stairways leading down to the stations, a provision for off-the-street access through the lobbies of buildings, plazas adjacent to them, or underground concourses was introduced. A law passed in late 1973 set up a transit-land-use district requiring that all new development located within one hundred feet of the projected subway stations, private or public, provide a transit easement. This easement area was to be used as an enlargement of the entrance to the subway to allow better access to it as well as to introduce light and air to the underground areas.

As it turned out, progress on the Second Avenue system has been halted. But the basic principle of the transit district has caught on in other cities and can apply to any development along a transportation system, above or below grade.

To improve transportation access points in other crowded areas, New York City uses incen-

The Porno Shop, 42nd St. New York City

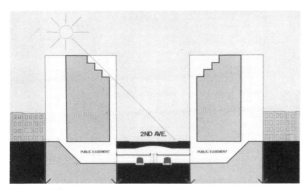

Second Ave., N.Y.C. Easement Concept

tive zoning, where major new buildings are developed above subway stops. In exchange for an increase in floor area, or a larger building envelope, the developer is required to provide a connection from his building to the subway, or else provide transit amenities in the form of escalators, elevators for the handicapped, or, in some cases, to allocate money for remodeling an adjoining station.

Analyze the transit needs along your street. Whether you require either additional parking, or more space in congested pedestrian areas around transportation centers, remember that there are zoning precedents for obtaining transit benefits in such places where new development is projected. You know best what transit or pedestrian improvements are most desirable along your street. If people arrive at your street by bicycle, think of how lovely it would be if in every new building bicycle racks were provided as a street amenity.

Zoning Affects Parking

The history of streets in the last quarter century has largely been the history of a clash — the one between cars and pedestrians. Even the most wonderful streets have been widened at the expense of sidewalks, trees, and landscaping. Streetlights and innumerable kinds of signs have been designed and positioned for the driver, not the pedestrian. The parking of cars (and double-parking of trucks) not only added to the pollution of streets and cut visibility of storefronts from one side of the street to another, but made life intolerable for people on foot.

In most cities, zoning includes parking provisions which vary depending on the use of the area. Residential, commercial, and manufacturing uses require allocation of different amounts of parking spaces. Zoning also may restrict the amount and location of parking permitted in certain streets and areas.

You want to determine the need and location for parking in future developments along your street as part of your parking policy. From the earliest moment that a development is projected for your street, you should establish a close and cooperative relationship with the agencies charged with traffic planning and urban design. This will give you a base for establishing a dialogue with the developer and his designers. Be prepared to spell out why it is in their best interest that such facilities as parking be handled in harmony with your street's planning objectives. You may prefer enclosed parking to open lots. Or, if you allow parking lots, you could specify where on the building site the parking should be. You might locate the parking lot in the back of the building rather than on the street frontage: Or else, your parking plan may mandate various methods of screening or landscaping the parking areas to minimize the visibility of the cars from the sidewalk.

Also, open parking lots which face the street tend to disrupt the continuity of shops and pedestrian activities. Instead, work out a provision whereby parking is accommodated within, under, or, as mentioned, unobtrusively behind a new building. If possible, discourage as much on-the-street parking as possible. Where on-the-street parking must exist for practical reasons, or where driveways to private garages access directly off the street and must be maintained, you might develop a zoning provision that spells out the number, general location, or possible clustering of parking lots or spaces, and identifies where entrances and exits to parking should be permitted or forbidden.

In New York City, curb cuts are limited to one for every building in high-density residential areas, and none at all are permitted along major retail streets, such as Fifth Avenue, Madison Avenue, and even Mulberry Street. The idea is simply to free the sidewalks as much as possible for the pleasure and safety of pedestrians. Furthermore, the evidence is more than ample, looking around the country, that there are practical and preferable ways to accommodate cars without using either open parking lots or chaotic on-the-street parking.

Zoning Reflects Environmental Care

San Francisco

As the creative dimensions of zoning have evolved in recent years, a number of tools have been developed to secure and augment the special visual and environmental qualities of cities, districts, and neighborhoods. The enactment of such zoning tools are a result of the general public's increased awareness that ''the environment'' includes more than just natural resources. A true concern for the environment deals with the relationships of buildings, streets, and other physical developments to the natural environment. Ideally, the built and the natural environments should feed off each other, complementing each other rather than being in a state of tension and conflict. Just as no element of nature exists alone, no building or street exists alone. In the same vein, a strong link exists between streets, entrances to buildings, buildings themselves, and the open spaces behind. It is imperative that any new development should relate sensitively to its surroundings.

In recent years, zoning methods have been written to protect the integrity of both the natural and man-made environments. Should your own street have a special relationship to such natural characteristics as hills, a riverfront, a harbor bay, or ocean shore — with a bracing view toward such a setting — you may want to consider proposing a zoning measure that would ensure that a new development along your street would not destroy the ''special relationship'' with its environment. The great architect, Frank Lloyd Wright, beautifully stated this principle when he said, ''A house

should never be on a hill at all, but of the hill.'' In the same spirit, any building or development should be of your street and of the vistas or other cherished landmarks that you can see from your street, and not impose obstacles to the enjoyment that people can derive from being there.

Zoning can help control the scale and height of new buildings and help preserve existing ones. Zoning mechanisms now in effect in a number of cities reflect this increased awareness. Perhaps the country's most noted precedent in controlling the configuration and scale of building is that of Washington, D.C. A visitor to the capital will notice a unique quality that goes beyond the individual monuments themselves. The predominant feeling can be attributed to the low scale that the city maintains with a strict hundred-and-twenty-foot-height limit on all developments. The exceptions, of course, are those buildings erected before the limit went into effect early in this century — the Capital, the Washington Monument, and a handful of others. Visual strength and continuity are further reinforced by the wide avenues and the green belt of the Mall which links the key monuments of the city.

However, such controls as height limitation have not been eagerly received by many politicians, developers, and businessmen. Such measures have been seen as a blanket denial of development rights. In the last few years, however, society has become more conscious and anxious about environmental issues. Citizens in a number of cities have begun to press for height and density limitations when faced with an uncoordinated and uncontrolled development which might mar the natural and visual aspects of their community.

One of the most prominent pioneer cities in environmental zoning is San Francisco. In 1972, concerned citizens pressured to mandate a sixty-foot-height limitation on new developments. These efforts failed but the strong civic sentiment caused city planners and officials to reassess the problem and bring back, years later, compromise height regulations which were implemented in 1979. These regulations were designed to reinforce the city's characteristic scale, its street patterns and, most crucial, the famous views through the streets to other sections of the city and more pervasively to the bay itself. In particular,

Cincinnati Hillside

building-height limitations were imposed: one hundred and sixty feet in San Francisco's central business district and forty feet in the surrounding sections of the city. The scale of the streetscape, especially as it relates to and celebrates the topography, is respected. New buildings are integrated with existing ones, giving identity, unity, and continuity to the cityscape.

Another example of environmental zoning is Cincinnati's mix of flexible design guidelines written in the zoning ordinance. Cincinnati is located on a basin of the Ohio River and is surrounded by hills. This physical setting truly gives the city a unique character, but it also accounts for a dichotomy between the natural and man-made environments. As development has increased over the past few years, citizens of Cincinnati have feared the destruction of its landscape. In reaction to their fear, development guidelines have been enacted. These guidelines don't discourage development, but instead encourage a more congenial relationship between old buildings, new buildings, and the contours of the hills. The guidelines provide for the preservation of hillsides and city views, ensuring that new developments will be of a close-grained, environmentally sound, low profile.

While San Francisco and Cincinnati and their distinctive features may seem remote from your own situation, the basic assumptions may be just what you can use for your community or street. Whether your city has 400,000 people or 40,000, the creative challenge of bringing development into harmony with existing buildings and streets is the same. And being familiar with the examples of Washington, San Francisco, and Cincinnati may guide you in developing tools for your own street.

Zoning Has Its Limitations

Because of all of the upbeat urban reforms of recent years, there is a temptation to think of zoning as the major redeemer of our cities' problems. Indeed, creative zoning has stimulated basic improvements in many downtowns across the country. But one must be very wary of assigning zoning too exaggerated a role, for its potential must always be regarded in terms of factual situations. Real estate trends, changing economic and social forces, shifts in population trends, the impact of density on the issue of enforcing zoning and related land-use laws — all these must be considered when asking what zoning can and cannot do.

Clearly, in revitalizing rundown areas like the South Bronx, where added densities are not sought by the developers, the role of incentive zoning is greatly limited. In such areas, the use of other devices such as major subsidies and tax incentives are required. Incentive zoning is most effective in areas where additional densities are sought and where the wish to provide amenities is only an added extra premium to an already economically vital area. Here, a major trade can be made which provides a public amenity in exchange for added floor area. But this additional density in high-built areas has not gone unnoticed by the communities in Midtown Manhattan or downtown San Francisco. In both places, a growing concern on the part of civic groups was voiced as to the adverse impact of this concentration.

Photo Montage of Possible Density in Manhattan

Another problem with incentive zoning is that an increase in density may jeopardize the quality of a newly created amenity. After all, an enlarged building which provides a plaza in exchange for more bulk may be so big that it blocks any sunlight from that plaza. Also, current real estate trends which develop buildings on smaller sites in order to preserve adjoining existing structures, in turn, prompt new tools such as lot mergers and transfer of air rights. While such tools may be effective in preserving buildings, they often result in a concentration of bulk, which is out of character with the whole neighborhood.

By now the fact has been established that there are ways for you to receive public amenities which benefit your own street. However, the word "amenity" does not always imply a quality amenity. In the New York experience, introducing just the word "plaza" into the zoning legislation seldom produced a worthwhile open space. Therefore, to discourage the resulting concrete strips of plaza in the city, a detailed list of landscaping and locational criteria had to be included in a special Urban Open Space document. You too may seek to develop rules for improving open space or storefront signage. Remember, however, that the more detail you include the more enforcement you need. Also, a maze of bureaucratic rules eventually may limit freedom in design.

Requirements should be simple and clear. A straight-forward approach will simplify your enforcement task. If, however, you depend on performance standards rather than on specific regulations, the task of determining what conforms is more complex and requires a more elaborate enforcement procedure. For example, it is easier to enforce a regulation that says "the building must be thirty feet high" as opposed to "the building must relate to the building next door." The latter requires hired professionals to interpret what conforming to the adjoining building means.

Entrance Sign to Covered Public Space Olympic Tower, N.Y.C.

Regardless of the approach, it is clear that most amenities are not completely maintenance-free. Look for a watchdog for your street. In New York City, the voluntary assistance of the community was sought and, therefore included in the zoning rules of a public open park mandatory signs announcing the hours of operation along with the name and number of the owner responsible for parks maintenance. A government contact for complaints was named, and sure enough, the community was fast to react.

Performance Bond— Part of Urban Open Space Leg., N.Y.C.

27-44 Performance Bond

Prior to obtaining any Certificat ings, the *building* owner shall p York, a performance bond or planting, movable seating, bicyc maintenance of the *residential* bicycle parking facilities and p the *development*.

The value of the bond or City shall be at a rate of $400 per r per 1,000 square feet of *resident* Section.

In the event that the Departme Chairman of the City Plannin determination whether there ha

An added enforcement control in New York is a bond posted by the owner with the city to cover the cost of replacing trees in the event that the owner forecloses on his responsibility. Pedestrian spaces located at the base of a building within private property cause a different enforcement problem. Every one of the covered pedestrian spaces recently built in Manhattan is open to the public during the day and closed for security reasons at night. Enforcing the hours of openness and the public accessibility to the space is difficult and costly. It is obvious that the more visible the amenity is from the street, the easier it is to control.

Finally, all of the zoning laws in the world cannot ensure good architecture. Even in Savannah's historic district, where strict controls mandate materials and colors and relate scale of new buildings to the existing ones, the architecture that results is not always distinguished. Two things are crucial to remember, therefore, as you attempt to solve your street's problems: zoning is no magic wand and there is no one simplistic solution.

HISTORIC PRESERVATION LAWS

Preservation is no longer a noble option. It has become a practical working ethic in American society. It has moved far beyond the stage where it was exclusively the enterprise of the rich, who fought to protect their mansions and clubs.

While the preservation of an isolated landmark is important, the forerunner of this type of preservation was the designation of. historic districts which began in the 1930's with such areas as Nantucket, Massachusetts and the Vieux Carré (the heart of old New Orleans). Since then, in addition to the increased federal, state and local laws that permit the designation of individual landmarks, the number of historic districts has also been greatly expanded. If your street is part of such a district, its buildings and area improvements may qualify for landmark funds from preservation-oriented government-grants programs. At the same time you should realize that such funding sources may place strict conditions on the kinds of reconstruction that can be made, often specifying the architectural details of the improvement and restricting flexibility in development. Sometimes, you may want to avoid the lengthy paperwork involved in receiving a small amount of money.

The extent to which a building or neighborhood is preserved may vary from city to city. In Savannah, Georgia, and Charleston, South Carolina, historic preservation covers major parts of the city. In cities like Boston and New York, smaller neighboring areas such as Beacon Hill and Greenwich Village are designated as historic districts. These districts represent one or more periods or styles of architecture exemplary of the city's history.

The irreplaceable loss, for people of small and large cities alike, of uprooting areas through the destruction of an area's unique aesthetic character or demolition of its distinctive buildings may adversely affect the economic strength of the city. This realization accounts for the great number of preservation laws across the country which reflect not only the desirability of improving landmarks but emphasize the importance of the economic feasibility of maintaining them.

Historic Districts

Gramercy Park
Historic District,
New York City

Historic districts are areas designated because of their distinct architectural style and character.

In New York City there are general rules governing historic districts such as Gramercy Park and Brooklyn Heights. Guidelines in these areas are limited to height restrictions, a review of the exterior of the building and of the interior to the extent that it affects the building's exterior. The Landmarks Preservation Commission determines that the design is appropriate to the area, on a case-by-case basis. In other parts of the country, historic districts contain more detailed requirements. In Old San Diego, a Control District Ordinance was adopted in 1966 with the objective of maintaining that area's appearance and character of 1871 and before. Height limitation of three stories was imposed and such architectural details as lighting, street furniture, landscaping, roof slopes, and materials were noted; the adobe tiles, colors, and textures that were mandated reflect the historic Spanish Mexican theme.

Within the historic district of Old Philadelphia, three hundred and thirty-nine buildings, mainly eighteenth-and nineteenth-century structures, are individually designated. In recognition of the historic importance of the area, the entire Old City was listed in the National Register of Historic Places as a historic district in 1972. In Philadelphia, as in New York, designation is done individually on a building-by-building basis. The Philadelphia Historical Commission reviews each design within the historic district and also provides advice on restoration guidelines. These guidelines are based on a hierarchy of possible building treatments within the district. Some buildings are designated because of their value as part of the street-scape, meriting merely conservation and adaptation for reuse; others are individual landmarks deserving of architectural preservation or restoration. On the other hand, in Ipswich, Mass., regulations of historic properties are accomplished by a voluntary program of facade and interior covenants which regulate changes made to a certified building.

Montague St.
Brooklyn, N.Y.C.

Landmarks

The New York City Landmarks Preservation Law demonstrates the extent to which preservation laws have been integrated into local legislation. The landmark legislation is administered by a chairman and a ten-member commission appointed by the mayor, and is part of the administrative code of the city.

Surprisingly, the Landmarks Preservation Commission of New York City was only established in 1965. Prior to this date, New York, like many other cities, had lost much of its irreplaceable heritage as priceless individual buildings were demolished. Fortunately, with the establishment of the commission, the destruction of significant buildings has been slowed down. The commission reviews each building with regard to its special character, aesthetic and cultural qualities, and its value in enhancing and stabilizing the cultural, social, and economic framework of the city.

The landmark law applies to any building that has been designated and that is at least thirty years old and meets the criteria, thereby meriting landmark status. Any construction, reconstruc-tion, alteration, or demolition of any improvement in a historic district or a landmark building is then subject to the landmark law. A landmark can be publicly owned, like City Hall, a commercial building like Grand Central Station, or privately owned like the famous Dutch Colonial-style Lent House in Queens.

In 1973, the law was amended to encompass interiors of structures and scenic landmarks. Thus, the four designations of the landmark law, individual buildings, historic districts, interiors, and scenic landmarks complement each other. One recently notable designation was that of the interior of Radio City Music Hall, an act which may have been responsible for saving that building. The "scenic landmark" designation applies to landscaped areas of special historical or aesthetic interest which are located on city-owned property. One preserved scenic landmark is the world-famous Olmstead masterpiece, Central Park.

Good intentions of preserving landmarks should be coupled with a financially realistic plan. While preserving and rehabilitating existing buildings often involve greater savings than building new ones, they can also entail major restoration which can be quite expensive. Restoration of fine architectural details and the heating and cooling of immense spaces are some of the economic constraints in landmark preservation. Also, constitutional rights require that the designation of a landmark not be deemed a "taking" of the owner's personal property. For these reasons, New York's landmarks law includes a hardship relief procedure, applicable to both individual landmarks or buildings within a historic district.

When an owner of a landmark in New York is able to demonstrate an economic hardship, the

Lent House, Queens
New York City

Landmarks Commission must develop a plan to relieve such hardship or else seek condemnation by the city. Short of such a plan, at the end of approximately one year, the owner can demolish the building or alter it appropriately. The relief plan could include real estate tax benefits, zoning changes, or a transfer of air rights; the commission might seek alternate uses for the building or attempt to find a purchaser who would preserve it.

Since its establishment, the Landmarks Commission has been successful in assisting owners to preserve their buildings. There have been occasions, however, where landmarks were demolished, such as the Jerome Mansion on Madison Square, famous as the home of Winston Churchill's grandfather. In this case, the owners were not making the proscribed reasonable return on the building, and the commission failed to devise a successful plan to save the mansion.

The recent Supreme Court Decision in favor of the landmark status of Grand Central Station has set an important precedent in support of preservation. The Court ruled that the landmark law did not interfere with the operation of the station in any way, and that the railroad failed to prove that it was not receiving a reasonable rate of return on the station as it was. Further, the Court found that the Landmark Preservation Law was a valid form of land-use regulation. This ruling, therefore, established the value of the law and has proven that, at all levels, the Landmarks Preservation Law is accepted as an important piece of urban legislation. While supporting the concept of preservation, officials in a recent National League of Cities meeting expressed their concern that preservation ordinances too often were used to try to stop new developments. This is clearly not the intent of this far-reaching law.

Radio City Music Hall, N.Y.C.

National Register of Historic Places

The National Register of Historic Places is the official list of the nation's cultural resources including districts, architecture, and objects significant in American history that are identified as important assets to be saved from destruction, damage, or decay and are eligible to receive protective and economic benefits.

It is administered by the Secretary of the Interior who, under the mandate of the National Historic Preservation Act of 1966, is authorized to establish the list and to approve grants to assist the states in preparing comprehensive surveys of such properties.

Nominations to the National Register are made at the state level by State Historic Preservation officers appointed by the governors. A state review board, whose membership includes professionals in the fields of architecture, history, and archaeology, approves each submission. There are, at present, about 700,000 individual buildings listed around the country. Places such as Historic Annapolis, in Maryland, and Hudson, New York, are examples of cities with large districts on the National Register. Being listed in the National Register of Historic Places may provide great benefits to your street or city. Here are some advantages that make it desirable to be listed on the National Register:
● It makes private property owners eligible to be considered for federal grants-in-aid for historic preservation through state programs.
● It provides protection for structures and places by requiring comment from the Advisory Council of Historic Preservation on the effect of federally assisted projects on these resources.
● It makes owners who rehabilitate certified projects eligible for tax benefits.

Eligibility for many additional tax incentives and tax "write off" provisions is based upon either listing in the National Register or state or local historic district designations. Find out if your street or a building on your street falls within the criteria as described by the National Register of Historic Places, in order to determine whether you can profit from its benefits. The criteria defines the quality of structures and places that:

● are associated with events that have made a significant contribution to the broad patterns of our history; or

● are associated with the lives of persons significant in our past; or

● embody the distinctive characteristics of a type, period, or method of construction, or that represent a significant and distinguishable entity whose components may lack individual distinction; or

● have yielded or may be likely to yield, information important in history or prehistory.

Look very carefully at the quality of your street, to determine the significance of your buildings or of your entire district to see if it merits being on the National Register of Historic Places.

Transfer of Air Rights

Transfer of air rights

Every zoning lot contains an imaginary envelope of airspace which represents its maximum development potential.

The transfer of air rights is a zoning mechanism that permits the transfer of the unutilized airspace or the development rights to an adjoining development. It is used primarily as an incentive to the developer to preserve an existing building or open space—located within his site or on an adjoining one—that is deemed an important asset to the community.

Assume there is a church of great quality occupying an adjacent parcel where a new development is planned. One way to protect this church from demolition is to use the transfer of air rights which allows the unutilized airspace from above the church to be transferred to the new development. The developer can thus add to the space on his adjoining site, which he gained from above the church. He now has an incentive to preserve the church itself. A good example of the use of a

Philip Morris Bldg.
42nd St., New York City

transfer of air rights is the Philip Morris Building on East Forty-second Street in New York. In this case, development rights were transferred from Grand Central Station to the Philip Morris office building, in return for establishing a trust fund which is earmarked for maintenance of the landmark station.

There is a limited amount of bulk that you would want to transfer to a single site, however. After all you don't want to dwarf the beautiful landmark you have just preserved by permitting the construction of a huge building that may cast a shadow upon it. In most areas of New York, the transfer of air rights from landmarks is limited to 20 per cent of the amount of the developable site, and includes a maintenance program in which the developer participates.

You may want to delineate an area of your street for preservation from which you will permit the transfer of bulk to another area. The major stumbling block here, however, is to find an area that will welcome such an additional density.

Facade Easements

One financial technique often used in historical preservation is a revolving fund which makes money available to purchase critical historical buildings for eventual resale to sympathetic new owners, or as a money-lending device for restoration or rehabilitation. Publicly or privately operated, this direct-acquisition technique may be often too expensive an undertaking.

Where government funds are unavailable or insufficient to acquire the property or relocate tenants and then improve the building, facade easement is the legal tool which enables government to apply for public money to improve and benefit private property, without confiscation. This technique is particularly useful in areas where buildings of great merit are privately owned by people who do not have the ability and means to renovate or restore their property.

The application of this innovative tool is becoming common around the country. Hudson, New York, is a good example of one of the first extensive uses of facade easement. There, many of the architectural high-quality buildings are located in areas primarily of low- and middle-income residents. Mandatory regulations to restore those buildings would have meant penalizing the property owners and driving them out of the vicinity. This was prevented by the facade-easement approach, which permitted the Hudson Urban Renewal agency to take easements, with the owners' approval, and rehabilitate the exteriors of their buildings. The owners, at their own expense, did likewise to the interior and further agreed not to make any changes on the outside without the city's approval.

Different government or other public bodies may be the recipients of facade easements, but in all cases approval of the owner is necessary. It is not uncommon that the community will retain an easement on a property to insure that there would be no adverse alteration in the future. In Yreka, California, as in Cohoes, New York, the city has

Facade Easement
Cohoes, New York

the right to control the exterior appearance of the property, notwithstanding alterations, new construction, and even colors and materials. In Yreka, the agency that holds the easement assumes the obligation of the facade improvements, yet the private owner is responsible for the maintenance of his property.

There are several benefits from the use of facade easements to the private owner. First, the improvement of the building increases the value of his property. Also, there are many tax benefits that are available in forms of decreased real estate taxes, or eligibility of government grants. In Philadelphia, owners of buildings may donate the right to control the visual appearance of their facades to a new nonprofit corporation, the Philadelphia Historic Preservation Corporation. An owner is then eligible to claim a charitable deduction of his federal taxes for the appraised value of the easement. In this case the easement is to be given for perpetuity.

Facade Easement
Philadelphia

The major benefit to the government of using facade easements is its ability to use public funds, such as community development money, which are otherwise prevented from being used to improve privately held buildings. This is the way building restoration is funded in the most complicated and far-reaching program of facade improvements in Salem, Massachusetts, as well as in Historic Annapolis.

In Historic Annapolis, the easement legislation is not limited to facades or historic districts but extends to entire buildings and to nonarchitectural areas and vacant land, in order to surround and protect the historically significant areas. The city feels that the use of easements is a better tool for both preservation and improvement of buildings than zoning is. Through the administration of a private preservation organization, more adequate attention is given to restoration and to design details than a public body often can give.

As far as compliance with easement regulations, experience demonstrates that since the easements are concentrated in small areas, and are usually done with the owners' consent, the owners tend not to violate the easement terms.

Along your street the innovative tool of facade

easement or easements in general may be a way for you to involve a government body or a preservation agency to help channel public money into the improvement of private property.

Restoration and Rehabilitation Techniques

When you launch a preservation effort along the street, you should determine what technique of preservation you should use. There are two basic categories into which preservation falls: restoration and rehabilitation.

Restoration is a process by which a building of great architectural quality is returned to its appearance at a specific point of time. If the quality of buildings along your street is as distinguished as in Williamsburg, or if they are on the National Register, you obviously want to apply a restoration technique. Also, every historic district has certain critical buildings reflecting the most essential historical spirit of the buildings. These probably should be restored. The advice of your landmark commission, the National Trust, or your local preservation group will assist you in determining the quality of the building and the extent of the work required.

The intricate detailing and craftsmanship make restoration more expensive than rehabilitation. These tasks require professional help. The work also may involve research to discover the exact appearance of the building when first constructed.

A technique more economical than complete restoration is rehabilitation. In the process of rehabilitating, the building is remodeled, with respect to its architectural integrity, without necessarily restoring every detail in accurate historical terms. In the course of rehabilitating a street, the scale and character are maintained, while flexible,

Eleventh Street
New York City

practical ways are used to deal with the interiors. Buildings are converted to other uses, employing modern techniques and contemporary materials. Historic restoration or rehabilitation may be done in phases, depending on the interest and the economic ability of individual owners and the availability of government grants. One advantage of rehabilitation is that often cleaning, painting, and placement of new signs can be handled by local contractors. More extensive work will require hiring an architect who is familiar with preservation techniques. While the street facade may appear to be relatively well maintained, the inside of the structure and the sidewalls may be crumbling. In some cases, owners want to opt for partial restoration such as bringing back the facade to its original appearance and charm, while carrying out rehabiliation, or even complete modernization, inside.

Whether you address a building or a whole street, don't copy history, unless there are overriding historical elements to preserve, by adding quaint colonial details to twentieth-century buildings. Strike a balance between modern times and the old charm. The architectural features of the older structures may inspire new creative ways to articulate the street qualities that you are so eager to preserve.

This is the case in Market Street, in Corning, New York, where an excellent example of rehabilitation work is part of the revitalization program of the business district. Also, what is now becoming a classic, the Quincy Market in Boston, is an extraordinary case of both restoration and rehabilitation which triggered the revitalization of a whole area. Whatever the technique you use, remember that immediate stabilization is essential for all long-term preservation, rehabilitation, or restoration.

These days, there are many lists of do's and dont's about rehabilation from the National Trust for Historic Preservation to the Heritage Conservation and Recreation Service. One such list of guidelines from the National Park Service, out of which the Heritage Conservation and Recreation Service was carved in 1977, is still of the best, most encompassing, and yet simple:
● Every reasonable effort should be made to provide a compatible use for buildings which will re-

quire minimum alteration to the building and its environment.

- Rehabilitation work should not destroy the distinguishing qualities or character of the property and its environment.
- Deteriorated architectural features should be repaired rather than replaced whenever possible.
- Distinctive stylistic features or examples of skilled craftsmanship, which characterize older structures and often predate the mass production of building materials, should be treated with sensitivity.
- Many changes to buildings and environments which have taken place in the course of time are evidence of the history of the building and the neighborhood. These changes may have developed significance in their own right, and this significance should be recognized and respected.
- All buildings should be recognized as products of their own time. Alterations to create earlier appearances should be discouraged.
- Contemporary design for new buildings in old neighborhoods and additions to existing buildings or landscaping should not be discouraged if such design is compatible with the size, scale, color, material and character of the neighborhood, building or its environment.
- Whenever possible, new additions or alterations to buildings should be done in such a manner that, if they were to be renovated in the future, the essential for and integrity of the original building would not be impaired.

Further echoing the interest in preservation in cities and towns across the country, the National Trust for Historic Preservation developed the far-reaching "Main Street" project which is designed to demonstrate (among other things) that preservation is a crucial component of commercial revitalization and to encourage small municipalities and urban neighborhoods to restore the economic, social, and aesthetic integrity of their central business districts. "Main Street" is presently applying and implementing these techniques in three cities (Galesburg, Illinois, Hot Springs, South Dakota, and Madison, Indiana). You can learn from their successes and failures, and from their extensive knowledge in the field of preservation.

Always remember that the keystone to any restoration or rehabilitation effort is the involvement of a strong nonprofit constituency.

FINANCIAL TOOLS AND INCENTIVES

One of the keys to the success of your street is knowing the financial resources that are available to you. The complexity of a street project often requires using more than one tool or program, the establishment of a financial committee, or the input of a knowledgeable banker or financial expert. Here are some basic tools for you to know about:

Direct Government Help

There are federal subsidies and programs that could assist you in financing your street improvement project. These programs change constantly; amounts are reduced and increased. Be familiar with what could apply to your street improvement. Today, such programs include Section 8 Housing Subsidies, Community Development Block Grants, Urban Development Action Grants, Department of the Interior grants-in-aid for preservation projects, Small Business Administration loans, Department of Commerce Section 312 loans, and UMTA loans. These programs often require matching funds from private resources. When no federal assistance is forthcoming, a private developer involved in a project, seeking to avoid project delays and a great number of reviews by outside agencies, may pursue tax incentives.

Tax Incentives

Tax incentives are designed by government to stimulate and attract development activities. Since about 20 per cent of the total gross income cost goes to cover real estate tax, it is obvious that abatement represents a powerful incentive tool. The incentives can be direct, such as those used to reduce taxes, assessment districts or local development corporations. Other incentives, classified as indirect, include the ability to reduce the cost of financing public sector activities through the sale of tax-exempt securities, as well as a variety of federally authorized tax incentives which will reward the developer for undertaking a public service project or for undertaking a private development that includes a public component.

Tax Abatement: Tax abatement is used to encourage development in areas which require public inducement to areas which fail to attract private investment. The Missouri tax abatement law, for example, is designed to encourage developers to make their own acquisitions, and permits the land to be taxed on its assessed valuation at the time of purchase and to remain at that level for the first 10 years. In addition, for the first 10 years, no taxes are paid on improvements. For the next 15 years, the land is taxed at its true assessed valuation and the improvements at an amount not to exceed 50 per cent of true assessed valuation. At the twenty-five year point, land and improvements are taxed at true assessed valuation

Some tax abatement programs don't apply specifically to a geographic area but rather to a use or purpose that government wants to encourage. In New York, for example, the J51 program is abatement intended to stimulate the conversion of

Building under J51 Program N.Y.C.

commercial buildings to housing. The J51 program like many others works on a sliding scale over the years and ranges from no taxes at the first year to full taxes at the end of the abatement period.

The tax abatement mechanism applies in specific situations to improve an adjoining area or building. This was the case when a tax provision was devised for the owner of the Commodore Hotel in New York. In exchange for attractive tax benefits the owner agreed to improve mass-transit connections, provide funding for rehabilitation of the adjoining Grand Central Station, as well as pay for the paving along Forty-second Street.

Tax Incentives for Preservation: Attractive tax provisions are now available for the rehabilitation and preservation of historic buildings. The Tax Reform Act of 1976, which is jointly administered by the Department of the Interior and the Department of the Treasury, has stimulated the use of individual historic properties that are listed under the National Register of Historic Places by offering tax incentives for rehabilitation and renovation. The incentives resulting from this act have sparked much interest in development circles for both large- and small-scale projects. According to the Heritage Conservation and Recreation Service, the bureau responsible for these preservation programs, 2,000 historic projects located in 46 states, varying from schools to churches, office buildings to housing, have been approved or are in some stage of the approval process to receive tax benefits in a two-year period.

The federal tax provisions include a five-year write-off to allow rehabilitation expenses which can apply to the interior and exterior of the building. The second provision allows for use of accelerated depreciation of the adjusted basis plus rehabilitation cost. The third incentive available is a 10 per cent investment tax credit for buildings twenty years or older.

Eligibility to the tax provision, which is based upon being listed in the National Register of Historic Places, can also apply to state or local historic district designations provided they are approved by the Secretary of the Interior. Where, prior to 1976, developers received write-off benefits for building demolition, since the passage of this tax reform no tax deduction for demolition costs of historic buildings has been granted. The Tax Reform Act also discourages the demolition of historic structures by denying any accelerated depreciation on new construction on a site of a building where a certified historic structure was demolished or substantially altered.

While new uses for historic structures vary, more than half of the projects involve the conversion of buildings into housing units. Since many of them are for subsidized housing, they involve direct and indirect housing subsidies. This is the case in downtown Hartford, Connecticut, where a massive housing rehabilitation project involving fifty buildings and a major private investment is underway using historic preservation tax write-off as a means of raising equity for the project from private investors.

Flour Mill, a mixed housing-, office-, retail-use project in the Georgetown Historic District, includes the adaptive reuse of the 19th-century brick Bomford Mill. This project, which includes the major rehabilitation of the two historic mill buildings, was made feasible by the extensive federal tax incentives.

The five-year write-off provision was also what sparked the interest of private owners to undertake the recycling of the Bellevue-Stratford Hotel, an early 20th-century landmark in Philadelphia, into the new Fairmont Hotel.

While many private developers may choose not to pursue tax incentives because of the number of reviews involved, tax incentives are clearly becoming a most useful tool in urban areas. With a current trend toward conservation and increased concern of people in preserving their links with the past, tax incentive for preservation purposes becomes more and more attractive.

Restored Fairmont Hotel

On your own street you may have one major building, a historical gem, or a whole facade that may be eligible for such benefits. Securing tax benefits and incentives is an effective way to enlist the interest of private financial support.

Tax Assessment District

A special tax assessment district is a designation given to a specific area which is planned for, or is undergoing, street and public improvements. Designating such a district assists the city in building and maintaining areas which otherwise its budget can neither initially afford nor continue to maintain.

Any street improvements affect the value of the properties along the street and subsequently increase the assessed tax of the property. The tax difference between the tax assessment before and after street improvement is made is called tax increment. This increment in the form of a special tax assessment is imposed by government upon the group of property owners in the area, to defray in whole or in part the cost of upgrading the operations of the streetscape. The tax increment goes into a fund which helps supplement the cost of operation and maintenance of the improvement.

While its application to streets around the country has been primarily used where new malls have been developed, the funds can also be used to subsidize restorations and rehabilitation of structures that economically may otherwise be marginal or unfeasible.

The great advantage of an assessment district is that it permits the use of funds that are kept apart from the general budget of the city and instead are reserved and directed to the specific area.

For an area to qualify as an assessment district, the legislative body of the state has to be convinced that the city cannot afford to improve the area without the use of such a tool. In New York City, the special tax assessment district is implemented through state legislation. Once it is approved, the special assessment is implemented and sanctioned yearly by the Board of Estimate.

Fulton Street in Brooklyn, 165th Street in Jamaica, Queens, and Nassau Street in Lower Manhattan are all pedestrian malls, involving the power of special assessment districts. This mechanism helps them to maintain their street as well as control sign regulations and all design matters.

In Yreka, California, the special assessment on Manor Street helps direct money to the street from the Parking and Business Act of 1965, which allows the levying of general business taxes directly to improve public-spaces events and retail activities.

If your street requires a major maintenance plan, and you can demonstrate to your legislative body the public benefits of establishing an assessment district, you may use this mechanism for upgrading your own street.

Bond Sales

In many areas around the country authorized programs by state and local governments will finance capital projects through the sale of tax-exempt bonds. Because they are tax-exempt, these bonds have been readily accepted by investors. The use of tax-exempt financing has been quite successful and most likely will continue to be a major element of support in funding capital projects of states, cities, and local communities.

The use of tax-exempt bond techniques varies from place to place. For example, in Portland, Oregon's downtown waterfront urban renewal area, state law and city charter permit payment of project costs through the use of increased property taxes resulting from the project. This is accomplished through the sale of urban renewal and redevelopment bonds to be paid off at a later date from rehabilitation and revitalization of the urban renewal area. Proceeds from the bond sale, which assist in financing the waterfront, were used to cover the development costs of a waterfront park, to assist in financing historic district projects, to acquire the sites of two parking garages, and to help in the acquiring of a site for a proposed transportation center.

Sometimes the bond issue is redeemed by assessing the value of the property and its location. This is the case of Nicollet Mall, in Minneapolis, where assessment of all property located within 330 feet of the Mall is based on the size frontage of the stores. Properties closest to the center of the Mall bear the greatest proportion of both construction and maintenance expense.

Since bond issues mainly apply to larger projects, it may not be a direct tool to use in a smaller-scale street improvement project. However, if the legislation to issue a bond is written to reflect the concern of neighboring communities, it is possible that modest but valuable sums can spin-off from that bonding capacity to help you refurbish your own street. What is important from your point of view is to find out whether your local government has the right to arrange for such financing and whether the source of funds is authorized for your project within the bonding capacity.

Private Financial Institutions

Most direct government funding programs require a long review process, and are subject to market interest rates. Since a major concern in financing your street-improvement project is the ability to borrow money at the lowest interest rate and to receive money on a timetable that allows construction to proceed as scheduled, the borrowing ability of private lending institutions (with or without the participation of the local government) is crucial.

The mechanisms and administration of these private bodies will vary with the circumstances and location. Bank consortiums, nonprofit organizations, and development corporations are vehicles to secure private funds below market interest rates for community-related projects. Often a revolving fund is used to channel such money to the community.

The revolving fund, usually administered by a private nonprofit organization, is a mechanism used to make money available for development projects with minimum delay. It is called a revolving fund because the money, when repaid, circulates directly back into the fund and so is readily available for additional projects. Since revolving funds circumvent lengthy budget-approval procedures, they have become extremely popular throughout the country. The first such high-risk revolving fund, the Neighborhood Services Fund, which was established in Pittsburgh in the late Sixties with seed money from two private foundations, has been extremely successful in providing funds for the rehabilitation of housing. Since then, 90 cities around the nation have followed suit, and are utilizing revolving loan funds for Neighborhood Housing Services.

The revolving fund is also very effective in expediting financing for restoration and preservation of buildings. In Seattle, Boston, and Pittsburgh, historic and landmark groups receive money from a variety of sources both private and public, and

implement their programs through a revolving fund.

Be thorough in searching for private financial institutions in your area that can help you in funding your project within your means. You may even decide to create your own revolving fund. This may be the key to getting your project off the ground.

IMPROVING DESIGN QUALITY

Architectural Review Boards

There are intangible properties in architecture and art that cannot be enforced through legislation. While the size or height of a building can be quantified, its spatial and intrinsic qualities cannot.

If you want to attract the highest quality of architecture along your street, you may use an architectural review board made up of professional architects and art experts. The role of such a board, often in an advisory capacity, is to serve both in selecting architects as well as in reviewing new projects developed along the street. Such a board may exist already in your local area or else may be formed and selected by you. It should represent the best talent available to you. You may discover that the most renowned architects may refrain from serving on the board because of their interest in doing the projects themselves; serving as a board member may mean a conflict of interest. It would be advisable, therefore, to create a rotating board which limits a member's service, let's say, to a year or two, after which he also becomes eligible to undertake an architectural commission on your street. An architectural board can play an extensive role as in Portland, Oregon, or a more limited one, as found in Corning, New York.

In Portland, Oregon, a city known for its concern for architectural quality, the seven-member-volunteer Design Committee, appointed by the

mayor, is given a major role. The board consists of a member of the City Planning Commission, a member of the Metropolitan Art Commission, one citizen representing the public at large, and four members experienced in either design, engineering, financing, construction or management of buildings, or land development. At least one member of this advisory panel must have considerable familiarity with Portland, while it is desirable for the others to have national urban design and development experience. Appointed by the mayor on a revolving membership basis, their terms are limited to four years.

In the downtown development zone and in other overlay design zones designated with the purpose of conserving and enhancing areas of special interest in the city, Portland's Design Committee, together with the City Planning Commission, is responsible for preparing guidelines for project evaluation and acceptability for consideration by the City Council. Once adopted by the council, these guidelines are utilized as a framework on all design review applications. The City Commissioner or the City Council may request and recommend that the Design Committee also review plans for areas outside the design zones on an advisory basis.

Since architecture cannot be quantified in absolute terms, encouraging a professional review board means risking objectivity in return for quality. In defining the role of the design review committee in Corning, New York, the question arose as to what design was good and what was "no good." The guidelines of the review committee eventually established that "no good" would be a "superstar scheme" rather than one that reinforces the character and scale of the composition that exists as a whole. It made clear from the start that the buildings would be expected to work in harmony and that no one building should be developed in isolation.

Old San Diego

In Old San Diego, a set of findings is established as a framework and give guidance for the review board to act upon. The basic standard of these controls specifies that all "forms, materials, textures and colors shall be in general accord with the appearance of the structures built in Old San Diego prior to 1871." The Architectural Control Board, appointed by the City Council, set design criteria regarding old, new, or restored buildings within the district.

Design standards are commonly used around the country not only as a basis for design review, but also as a directive to legislators, developers, and the community at large.

Design Guidelines

Design guidelines or standards can be part of a zoning ordinance or an administrative code. Whether they are mandatory or voluntary, they express policy on design matters and often set criteria for the design review board. An example of a mandatory guideline is the one in Portland, Oregon, which requires every parking garage to provide two levels of ground-floor retail. Voluntary guidelines are offered in Racine, Wisconsin, where a "design improvement file" for buildings,

storefronts, signs, window displays, and alleys was developed. The intent is "to bring visual order to physical elements without destroying the natural variety that is a necessary part of every commercial area". Racine Urban Aesthetics, Inc., which was responsible for developing the rules, emphasizes that they are guidelines, and not law.

Design standards apply to both development and preservation. They are not always incorporated in the legislative tools; sometimes they are published in the form of a report and then distributed around the community. Voluntary design standards permit greater latitude in design and architectural expression and eliminates the need for the enforcement of such delicate issues as color and texture. Yet, since voluntary standards are at the discretion of the owner they don't carry the weight of law.

In Cincinnati, flexible and mandatory guidelines complement each other. The city is divided into environmental-quality districts, each including a plan with attached flexible design guidelines representing the major feature of the district. In the business district, signs are limited to one business sign per establishment, and flashing signs are permitted on theaters only. However, the design of signs throughout the district is left to the judgment of the designer, provided it relates in character to the type of business and to the architecture of the building. The materials, colors, and textures should be harmonious with the surrounding buildings. Other guidelines applying to the business district relate building heights to existing buildings and to the preservation of open space.

Also in Cincinnati, the traditional Findley Market zone guidelines articulate the preservation of its nineteenth-century character. The use of traditional business signs and materials and the restoration of side porches and verandas are recommended. In residential neighborhoods, the guidelines emphasize the quality of life for its residents. Retail continuity, bus shelters at transportation nodes for inclement weather, and the coordination of parking entrances are required. Increase in lighting intensity along the street and landscape improvements around public areas help emphasize a better housing environment.

Design Guidelines
For Bay Windows
San Francisco

In San Francisco's residential areas, urban design criteria are used to make certain that new development is in character with the city's typical town house. One of the rules, for example, ensures the preservation of the topographic silhouette of San Francisco by requiring building roof lines and floor levels to step up or down with the slope of the site. Other design rules encourage bay windows and decorative features on the facade by allowing construction of continuous overhead projections above the existing sidewalk.

To form an architectural review board or develop design guidelines, you will need the assistance of professional architects and designers. They will add a dimension of quality to your street which you may never have imagined possible.

Quality Threads Throughout

Architectural review boards, design guidelines, and incentive zoning mechanisms are only as effective as their ability to translate fundamental objectives into reality. And that means not only improving the physical surroundings but also responding to the needs of the people living there and strengthening their staying power. As you strike a balance between using existing tools and developing new ones, don't neglect creative input which is a major force in reshaping your street. Indeed, the extent to which this dimension is integrated into your process, no matter how sophisticated or innovative the mix of tools becomes, will determine the success of your effort. Design quality, down to the most minor element of your overall program, will elevate the level of interest in your community and help you win the confidence of your neighbors. As you think of the future, remember that the way you apply the various innovative, legal, and funding tools will reflect your own values.

Practical tools and human passions can work together. As the renowned architect Louis Sullivan stated, ''...'practical' signifies explicit and implicit human needs. Such needs run a wide gamut of desire, ranging from the immediately physical and material, gradually upward in series through the desires of emotional, intellectual, and spiritual satisfaction.''

The fulfillment of his well-known dictum that *''form follows function''* has already been included in your approach to the street's daily workings. But the more meaningful sense of your intimate involvement, the deeper meaning to the functions that forms must follow, prevail throughout: Guiding you along your journey is the ethic that *''form follows care.''*

The spirit and joy that you bring to your process will help rebuild the qualities and values of your street's heritage and will become a living example for future generations to celebrate.

CREDITS FOR THE NEW YORK CASE STUDIES

URBAN DESIGN

Raquel Ramati, Director
Michael Parley, Deputy Director
Patrick Ping-tze Too, Project Director
Rita Bormioli, Project Director (Little Italy Special District)

Elizabeth Errico, John Hart, Renée Kemp, Brunilda
Mesa, Merry Neisner, Frank Nicoletti, Susan Orsini,
Clifford Rodriguez, Dorothy Svitzer, Kuo ming Tsu,
Kanhubhai Vyas, Dora Zhivotinsky

LEGISLATION—LITTLE ITALY SPECIAL DISTRICT

Norman Marcus, Counsel
Pares Bhattacharji, Andrea Kremen,
Fred Zauderer, Holly Leese

PLANNING—NEWKIRK PLAZA

Harvey Schultz, Director, Brooklyn Office
Orville Romney, Deputy Director
Priscilla Ross, Project Director
Cornelia Schimert, Project Planner
Michael Weiss, Ed Fox, Jerry Sakowsky,
Michael Barry, Ronald Bertrand, Holly Kaye,
Anita Webb

PLANNING — BEACH 20TH STREET

William Donohoe, Director Queens Office
Frederick A. Lee, Project Director
Zachary Weiss, Planner
Nancy Humphrey, Jenny Morgenthau, David Love,
Frank Chin, Sidney Baumgarten, Pearle Appleman

Special thanks to former Mayor Abraham Beame,
former Chairman of the City Planning Commission
Victor Marrero, Commissioners Martin Gallent, Sylvia
Deutsch, Howard Hornstein, and Anthony Ameruso, and
Borough Presidents Percy Sutton, Donald R. Manes,
Sam Leone.

And of course major credit is due to the community
organizations and their dedicated members who helped
in implementing the three case studies.

PHOTO CREDITS

A NOTE ABOUT THE AUTHOR

Raquel Ramati has earned a national reputation as a leader in the field of urban design. As Director of the Urban Design Group of the City of New York from 1974 to 1980, she was instrumental in passing zoning legislation concerning urban open space, subway easements, sidewalk cafes and the preservation of neighborhoods in that city. Born in Tel Aviv and educated in Technion Haifa School of Architecture and Pratt Institute, Ms. Ramati has taught at several universities, including Harvard (where she was a Loeb Fellow), New York University, UCLA, and the University of California at Berkeley. She has also lectured and written widely on the topics of architecture, city planning and the politics of design. Ms. Ramati serves as the Mayor's Representative on the Art Commission of the City of New York, and she conceived the highly acclaimed photography exhibit "Celebration: New York in Color," which was displayed in shop windows on Fifth Avenue, and which is now on an international tour. A member of the Downtown Redevelopment Council of the Urban Land Institute, Ms. Ramati has won several professional awards, including the Municipal Art Society Award, the Progressive Architecture Award and an *Urban Design* Magazine award.